CENTRE FOR PENTECOSTAL THEOLOGY
NATIVE NORTH AMERICAN CONTEXTUAL
MOVEMENT SERIES

Consulting Editor
Corky Alexander

HOLY SMOKE
THE CONTEXTUAL USE OF NATIVE AMERICAN
RITUAL AND CEREMONY

HOLY SMOKE

THE CONTEXTUAL USE OF NATIVE AMERICAN RITUAL AND CEREMONY

CASEY CHURCH

Cherohala Press
Cleveland, Tennessee

Holy Smoke: The Contextual Use of Native American Ritual and Ceremony
Centre for Pentecostal Theology Native North American Contextual Movement Series

Published by Cherohala Press
900 Walker ST NE
Cleveland, TN 37311
USA
email: cptpress@pentecostaltheology.org
website: www.cptpress.com

Library of Congress Control Number: 2016956303

ISBN-10: 1-935931-60-1
ISBN-13: 978-1-935931-60-7

Available at special quantity discounts when purchased in bulk by bookstores, organizations, and special-interest groups.
For more information, please e-mail cptpress@pentecostaltheology.org.

DEDICATION

To My Mother and Father
Mary B. Church-Stevens-Pokagon, Pokagon Band of Potawatomi
And
Leonard Henry Church, Nottawasippi Band of Potawatomi

CONTENTS

FOREWORD

As believers in Jesus, we are expected – *commanded* – to '… go and make disciples of all nations, baptizing them in the name of the Father and of the Son and of the Holy Spirit' (Mt. 28.19). God sometimes stretches us by calling us into ministry to people from other cultures – other nations.

Holy Smoke is exciting, good news for those called to serve Native American and First Nations people – for that matter to anyone called to make disciples of all nations – all people from all other cultures.

Dr Casey Church (Potawatomi) and his wife Lora (Navajo) have decades of ministry experience among their own Native people. In this book, Casey describes Wiconi's Family Camp and Powwow – now the Richard Twiss Memorial Powwow in Turner, Oregon – as a 'living laboratory' for contextual ministry. He goes into detail about how he uses Native American ceremony and tradition there in Christ-honoring ways. Lives and entire families are changed as Indigenous people hear the gospel in their own cultural languages.

Casey also works with and consults for the Brethren in Christ Overcomers Alcohol Treatment Program in Farmington, New Mexico. He conducts Christian Sweat Lodge and Pipe ceremonies, provides guidance in contextual ministry methods, and gives instruction in how to conduct Native American ceremonies in ways that glorify Jesus.

The Brethren in Christ program's recovery rate ranges from 70-75%. I, a nurse, have been told by a secular alcohol rehabilitation counselor and a friend working in a Native American Community Wellness program that this success rate is remarkable – pretty much unheard of.

The inclusion – the reintegration of Native American cultural practices including Native-style music and dance – is an important part of people learning to know who they were created to be. Revelation 7.9 says, 'After this I looked, and there before me was a great multitude that no one could count, from every nation, tribe, people and language, standing before the throne and before the Lamb'.

Knowing who you were created to be is important, but Casey recognizes that faith in Jesus is primary; He holds all things together (Col. 1.17). Jesus at the center, as the 'head' of contextual ministry, is powerfully changing lives and nations.

My husband Ray and I were captivated by this glimpse into Native American traditions through Casey's descriptions. We want you to dive into the fascinating imagery in this book, learn about Native American cultural practices, and consider the possibility that families and generations can be transformed by the power of this Holy Spirit-saturated ministry style.

We invite you to search the concepts in this book, put them into practice, and join us on this journey! Use what you learn to change the world through the power of the gospel.

Sue and Ray Martell
Editors of *Rescuing the Gospel from the Cowboys: A Native American Expression of the Jesus Way* by Richard Twiss.

ACKNOWLEDGEMENTS

I would like to extend my gratitude to the Navajo Brethren in Christ Mission in Bloomfield, New Mexico, and their Overcomers Alcohol Treatment Program and staff for participating in my study. I also thank the many unnamed clients and other participants who filled out the questionnaires and offered their input, as well as the people who participated in personal or group interviews.

The research could not have been completed without the help of my instructors, Sherwood and Judith Lingenfelter. I appreciate their guidance and encouragement. They directed me to 'see myself as a leader' and encouraged me to develop my leadership skills.

My special thanks goes out to the many Wiconi International Family Camp attendees who helped by responding to the questionnaire. I would further like to say a *Migwetch* (thank you) to Ray and Sue Martell for editing this manuscript.

LIST OF TABLES

LIST OF ABBREVIATIONS

BICO	Brethren in Christ Overcomers
MN1V	Many Nations One Voice
MPI	My People International
NAIITS	North American Institute for Indigenous Theological Studies: An Indigenous Learning Community
UMC	United Methodist Church
WFC	Wiconi Family Camp

INTRODUCTION

WICONI INTERNATIONAL – THE LEGACY OF RICHARD TWISS

How do we begin to understand change and transition within the Native American world? Since 1492 the Native American world has encountered radical changes caused by many outside forces. Into a somewhat stable Native American world came newcomers ready to settle the land in *very* foreign ways with *very* foreign weapons. At first, the Native Americans lived among the newcomers, but soon diseases brought by the settlers spread like wildfire across North America. It is estimated that up to 90% of the New World's original inhabitants succumbed to disease. In those early contact years, both Natives and colonizers warred against each other over precious land wanted for new white settlements. In more recent times large numbers of Native American people were forcefully moved west of the Mississippi onto 'reservation' land. Trauma from the loss of traditional territory was compounded by the introduction of boarding schools. The schools attempted the removal of Native culture from Native people. A phrase coined at the time by Col. Richard Pratt, the designer of the Carlisle Indian School, was, 'Kill the Indian, save the man'.[1]

Making matters still worse was the Indian Relocation Act of 1956, which moved thousands of Native Americans from their

---

[1] Richard H. Pratt, 'The Official Report of the Nineteenth Annual Conference of Charities and Corrections, 1892', Reprinted in *The Advantages of Mingling Indians with Whites, Americanizing the American Indians: Writings by the Friends of the Indian 1880-1900* (Cambridge, MA: Harvard University Press, 1973), pp. 46-59.

reservations to cities, with the offer of jobs and housing. The program was a miserable failure. Change and transition have been a way of life for the Native people of the Americas, both North and South, and all other Indigenous people around the world.

Mission work among Native American people has taken place mostly on reservations – where it is and was wrongly assumed that most Native people live. But, according to the 2010 U.S. Census, only 22% of the people who self-identify as Native American, Alaska Native, or 'Multi-race Native', live on 'Native Indian areas' (reservations, traditional land, etc.). Those living 'outside Native areas' (urban and rural) amount to 78%.[2] Despite these statistics, the majority of mission work, both short and long-term, continues to take place on reservations. Throughout the Christian history of Native American missions, Native peoples' traditional lifestyles and religious beliefs have continually faced criticism, both from the government and religious organizations.

The late Dr Richard Twiss, cofounder with his wife Katherine of Wiconi[3] International, a contextual ministry, brought significant new vision, hope, and change to Native American people and churches. In his book, *One Church, Many Tribes*, Twiss said of Native Americans, 'They said they had been taught by Native and non-Native leaders alike that their cultural expressions were bad and demonic and needed to be rejected'.[4] These responses to our cultural ways have prompted many of us to seek better ways of creating culturally-appropriate methods of evangelism. Those attempting new approaches have met with personal and professional criticism from within *and* without religious denominations. Some have conceded to the pressure and backed down from their calling from God. Still, God has reserved a remnant of believers who are answering His invitation to move forward in creating contextual ministry methods.

Innovative leaders like Richard Twiss are the reason change began and still occurs. For many years now Native people attending churches in their respective communities 'chafe or gnaw at the bit'

---

[2] Richard Twiss, *Rescuing the Gospel from the Cowboys: A Native American Expression of the Jesus Way* (Downers Grove, IL: InterVarsity Press, 2015), p. 252.

[3] Wiconi (wuh-CHO-nee), 'life' in the Lakota language.

[4] Richard Twiss, *One Church, Many Tribes: Following Jesus the Way God Made You* (Ventura, CA: Regal Books, 2000), p. 1.

because the Western way of 'doing church' lacks meaning to them. They realize something has to be taken from them in order to be counted as believers. Concerning the use of Western forms of worship and liturgy, Twiss wrote:

> … sometimes the practice of [Western] rituals becomes so routine that people no longer know the meaning of the symbol, nor are they able to articulate the meaning to themselves or to outsiders. They long for the freedom to express themselves in innovative expressions created from within their ancestral traditions. They seem to connect to some collective consciousness that meets a long awaited need of special connection to their Creator.[5]

Those brave contextual innovators have a deep hunger to see their own communities and family members feel what they are experiencing spiritually. The changes and transitions in their lives have sometimes come at a very high cost – the loss of personal and professional relationships. I grew up going to 'camp meetings' in our region every summer. These tent revivals were only attended by those who wanted to worship in a Western tradition. They continue to attend because it fills their souls, but it is, in fact, a very ineffective way to reach the many Native people who are disaffected by these methods of evangelism. You may be doing a lot of things for God, 'But if you aren't increasing the kingdom and reaching those outside God's family and bringing in more people to become followers of Jesus, then you might as well fold up your tent and go home'.[6]

Twiss clearly articulates the need for change:

> … Malcolm McFee makes an attempt to measure 'levels of acculturation' among the members of the Blackfeet Indian tribe of northern Montana. As a result of his study he coined the phrase, 'the 150% man', to describe a person who is of mixed-blood ancestry. The 150% man is able to easily and freely move

---

[5] Twiss, 'Rescuing Theology from the Cowboys' (DMin, Asbury Theological Seminary, 2011), p. 128.

[6] Rick Richardson, *Evangelism Outside the Box: New Ways to Help People Experience the Good News* (Downers Grove, IL: InterVarsity Press, 2009), p. 19.

between his Native and white cultures to serve effectively as an interpreter between the two and on behalf of both.[7]

As the current Director of Wiconi International, I must have the ability to serve both my Native people and the non-Native people involved with the ministry. Living in both worlds makes me a 150% man and gives me the advantage and ability to use my gifts for God's glory more fully. The apostle Paul, being both a Roman citizen and a Jew, had the freedom to move back and forth between those very different cultural settings. As a cultural insider in each world, Paul claimed to be 'all things to all people in order that I might win some' (1 Cor. 9.22).

When my dear friend Richard Twiss passed on, Wiconi was left with the need for a director to manage the organization through the transition: either to close its doors or continue in ministry. The Wiconi leadership met and decided that it should continue as an active organization. At that meeting I volunteered to help work to make Family Camp happen that summer (2013). Before then, I had rarely spoken during the decision-making process, but at that point, I accepted the responsibility of making critical decisions for organizing the next Family Camp.

Just as Richard had gone through the process of finding his leadership voice, I had to do the same. I needed to find out how best to be an instrument to frame issues effectively, shape and tell stories purposefully, and inspire others to believe in the vision of the Wiconi founders. I strongly relate to Richard's desire to build the organization he had foreseen and spent his life fulfilling. The moment I received my vision from God, fulfilling it became the priority of my life. My personal interests had now given way to the 'marching orders' I received from God.

Some leaders in my situation choose to continue the status quo initiated by former leaders. During times of transitional leadership, newcomers must move within an organization's framework, but they can also be the catalyst for change. What good is vision, or what good are new ideas, unless the leader can help others see them?

---

[7] Twiss, 'Rescuing Theology from the Cowboys', p. 113.

Throughout his life and ministry, Richard shared his dream for a 'preferred future' with my wife Lora and me. He did this by inviting us to work at Wiconi Family Camp because as he saw it, we personified what a contextual family looked like. We want to inspire and encourage others to continue to move contextual ministry into the future.

My new position required me to take a long look at how I would fit in with the current Wiconi staff (soon to be my friends) as I was entering a phase of change, transition, and liminality. As I entered the first stages of transition I considered what should be changed and what new approaches would be needed. I was putting myself in 'construction' mode. I knew from my experience with carpentry that it takes more effort to remodel than it does to build something new. As a new leader, I was in a position to help create a new Wiconi. Part of my job was to help lead Wiconi through the changes and transitions we would encounter during this liminal time.

Richard's innovative approach to Native ministry has inspired me since the beginning of my ministry journey with him. It has not been an easy road, but it is the road I have chosen because of my disillusionment with the status quo in Native ministry.

Richard broke the mold of traditional approaches to Native American ministry and embraced the concept of 'retraditionalization'. 'Retraditionalization, then, is the ever-increasing understanding of reliance upon cultural beliefs, customs, and rituals as a means of overcoming problems and achieving Indian self-determination'.[8]

How Transition to Contextual Ministry Happens

Transition to a contextual ministry or organizational style does not just 'drop in your lap' – it takes the special ability of listening well.

Listen from your heart with curiosity and compassion beyond judgment, to understand the sources of people's distress over a proposed initiative. It is not enough to say, 'I hear what you are saying', or to repeat it back. Try to 'walk in their shoes' to feel

---

[8] Twiss, 'Rescuing Theology from the Cowboys', p. 38.

something akin to what they are feeling, and then tell them what you have come to understand. At the very least, you have to be able to say with credibility, 'I see'.[9]

But how can someone from a different ethnic and cultural background make appropriate changes for another people group?

As a cultural insider, I have the ability to walk in their shoes, see with their eyes, and feel with the heart as a Native Christian. The acceptance of contextual ministry methods has been a process. As discussed in Everett Rogers' *Diffusion of Innovations,* it began with innovators, progressed to early adaptors, and is now on the downside of Rogers' bell curve to the point where late adaptors are making their way into the ranks of the contextual ministry paradigm.[10] But the late adaptors need to be sensitive to the need for ministries that can effectively reach postmodern people. They need to realize that perceived needs are very important – 'needs for belonging, relationship, community, identity, spirituality and an experience of the transcendent'.[11] Richard had this type of sensitivity and was able to understand and help to create a ministry *for* Natives *by* Natives (Wiconi International).

These human needs are common to all people, but spiritual needs and viewpoints can differ from one culture to another. Paul Hiebert observes how cultures and religions have closer ties in some people groups than in others: 'In traditional cultures it is hard to draw a sharp line between religious and non-religious practices. In many societies religion is a core of the culture and permeates all of life.'[12] Many tribes, such as my own Potawatomi tribe, do not show a distinct division between the sacred (religion) and the secular (everyday). So as an insider (researcher) I live in two worlds at the same time.

---

[9] R.A. Heifetz, M. Linsky, and A. Grashow, *The Practice of Adaptive Leadership: Tools and Tactics for Changing Your Organization and the World* (Watertown, MA: Harvard Business Review Press, 2013), p. 266.

[10] Everett M. Rogers, *Diffusion of Innovations* (New York: Free Press, 2010), p. 392.

[11] Richardson, *Evangelism Outside the Box,* p. 87.

[12] Paul G. Hiebert and R. Daniel Shaw, *Understanding Folk Religion: A Christian Response to Popular Beliefs and Practices* (Grand Rapids, MI: Baker Publishing Group, 2000), p. 184.

This has led me to step back and ponder the way research has been conducted among Native people over the years. As insiders, we find it hard to treat Native people as research subjects – as mere sources of data. I am a Native person in a leadership role, and I have friendships with Wiconi staff and Family Camp attendees, and the Brethren in Christ Overcomers staff and clients. This project is *personal* to me and the research process can become very dehumanizing. Native people have been studied for years and years. Every generation of non-Native people wants to know more about Native people. The fascination with Native people is still strong and becomes even more so as the contextual movement grows. I struggled to handle this project's research as raw empirical data. This is not a new issue among Indigenous people involved in research. Beatrice Medicine, a Native researcher, has written about these concerns in her book, *Learning to be an Anthropologist and Remaining Native*. She says, 'Native populations are wary of others' interpretations of their behaviors, even when they are dealing with "one of their own"'. [13]

Taking Contextualization into the Future

Rites of Passage – the processes of transition, change, and liminality – take place within various situations in our lives. Change, transition, and liminality influence the ability of individuals and organizations to move forward. Native rituals and ceremonies used in a Christ-honoring way (and their part in the Rites of Passage) can be innovations that lead to creating new directions in ministry.

In my life story, I have done little on my part except to make myself available to be used by God. As a result, the Wiconi Board offered me a staff position as the Wiconi Family Camp Director. The next year, they asked me to become Director of Wiconi. I have been privileged to be a part of a growing contextual movement formed by a generation of young Native American ministry

---

[13] Beatrice Medicine and S.E. Jacobs, *Learning to be an Anthropologist and Remaining Native: Selected Writings* (Champaign, IL: University of Illinois Press, 2001), p. 5.

leaders increasingly disappointed with the ineffectiveness of the Western style of Christianity introduced to us in our youth.

Richard Twiss was the reason so many of us thrived in ministry. It was his leadership and vision that gave the inspiration that was just what the Native American contextual movement needed. Although it did not have an easy start, Wiconi eventually ran smoothly and became the hub around which we centered our own ministries. Now we have begun a new chapter in contextual ministry. With an ending, a new beginning arises. Over generations, Native people have gone through many such endings and beginnings. When transition happens and our lives are dramatically changed, we use the Native saying, 'Our circle has been broken and needs to be mended'. Native American lifeways and identities are continually under stress. To survive we must regain what we have lost of our world by redefining and reshaping what remains.

Working from within our current missional framework, we should build on our history and legacy but also show we are progressive and willing and able to face a new future. We need to create contexts for the Holy Spirit to awaken people to their spiritual longing and begin to see Jesus as the satisfier of this longing.[14] I believe neglecting this crucial step has been the missing link in our Western evangelistic strategy. We need to move more toward discipleship and spiritual development in the structure of our Native ministries. Innovation will be a part of creating the 'preferred future' for Native people.

Innovations and Influence

There are many interacting dynamics in any change and transition process. The clients at the Brethren in Christ Overcomers (BICO) Alcohol Treatment Program experience many of the same transitional challenges as Wiconi has. In reality, change, transition, and liminality are at work in most life situations. Progress happens as a result. As with the clients at the BICO ministry, and Wiconi staff members during the leadership transition, the intentional move to innovate creates an environment for constructing a new future.

---

[14] Richardson, *Evangelism Outside the Box*, p. 60.

The processes of change and transition the Overcomers program and the Wiconi ministry are going through are well-illustrated by Everett Rogers' work in the *Diffusion of Innovations*. Rogers looks at a group's acceptance of an innovation. Acceptance or rejection of any change is rooted, as I have observed, in a fear of the unfamiliar.

Learning about contextualization at Wiconi Family Camp helps to assist individuals who are in their own Liminal Phase (neutral zone) of cultural understanding.[15] Those of us who have more experience with contextualization are also in a Liminal Phase in that we are busy working within the challenge of creating a unique environment. When people are in the Liminal Phase of their journey at Wiconi Family Camp, they can experience being in the midst of a group in total acceptance of contextualization.

We can capitalize on the Liminal Phase by encouraging Family Camp attendees to innovate. We can also use this time of transition as a time ripe for opportunities to embrace new methods within the Wiconi organization itself. Instead of looking at this time as meaningless, we are able to think outside the box and explore avenues not tried before.

Conclusion

God has opened a door for me to step into full-time ministry with Wiconi and has provided the means to accomplish his work. You would think that someone would jump in running when presented with such an opportunity. I thought I would, but I took the time necessary to make a wise (and major) decision. Lora and I considered the offer of leadership at Wiconi with much reflection and prayer.

There are individuals from many backgrounds, ethnicities, and social standings working for the Lord. All, in their own special way, have sensed God's call on their lives. I have had the opportunity to meet many of the Lord's workers and I am convinced he truly loves diversity – therefore I am in good company!

---

[15] Alan Roxburgh, *The Missionary Congregation, Leadership, and Liminality* (New York: Bloomsbury Academic, 1997), p. 27.

Our personal histories shape us and make us all different. Our ministry callings take many forms. Each one of us knows Jesus deep inside of our heart and wants to serve him fully and whole-heartedly. He gives the gifts of evangelism, teaching, and preaching and – even to this carpenter hired as a new Wiconi director!

Beginnings are part of the process I have been working on thus far. For me they include rituals and ceremonies – or Rites of Passage. Leadership with Wiconi was not something I had planned, but was something I was prepared for by all my previous life situations and circumstances. Starting this new leadership path is just another ending/beginning, neutral zone/liminal phase, and beginning/ending that I am prepared to step into. Bridges explains starts and beginnings as follows:

> Starts take place on a schedule as a result of decisions, they are signaled by announcements. Beginnings, on the other hand, are final phases of this organic process that we call 'transition' and their timing is not set by dates written on a schedule. Beginnings follow the timing of mind and heart.[16]

My new life direction is causing me to pause and look back introspectively. The most important things to me now are: getting my children started in life in the right direction, my life with Lora as our family size grows smaller, and my new life work with Wiconi.

As I consider past work, I believe my colleagues and I have done the Lord's work by laying the foundations of contextual ministry. I (among others) am now convinced of the need to teach people 'how to do' contextual ministry by using my own personal experience as a pastor, the director of Wiconi, a cultural consultant for the Brethren in Christ Overcomers Alcohol Treatment Program, and through the example of the work started by Dr Richard Twiss and his wife Katherine.

---

[16] William Bridges, *Transitions: Making Sense of Life's Changes* (Boston, MA: Da Capo Press, 2009), p. 58.

1

RITUAL PROCESS AND CHANGE – MY PERSONAL STORY

I am a Pokagon Band of Potawatomi member from Southwest Michigan. My Potawatomi name is *Ankwawango*, which means 'Hole in the Clouds'. I am of the Bear clan from my mother's side, (the late Mary Church-Pokagon, a Pokagon Band Potawatomi member) and the Crane clan from my father's side (the late Leonard Church, Nottawasippi Huron Band of Potawatomi). My wife Lora (Navajo) and I are raising five children in Albuquerque, New Mexico, where we have lived since 2000. My journey in Native American contextual ministry has created a desire for me to study under elders from whom I learned many of the traditional spiritual teachings of my Anishinaabe people of the Great Lakes region. I have a Bachelor of Science degree in Anthropology from Grand Valley State University in Allendale, Michigan, where I studied the culture and religion of Native American peoples. I also have a Master of Arts and a Doctor of Intercultural Studies from Fuller Theological Seminary in Pasadena, California, where I studied culturally-appropriate approaches to Christian theologizing in the Native American context (contextualization).

Lora and I pastored a Native church plant in Grand Rapids, Michigan, from 1996 to 2000, during which we offered one of the first contextualized worship services in the country. We have also led Native Christian ministries in the Southwest, where we continue to minister today.

I have been a presenter at national and regional conferences dealing with Native ministry topics. Currently, I minister with the

Brethren in Christ Overcomers Alcohol Treatment Program near Farmington, New Mexico, where I conduct a Christ-centered contextual Sweat Lodge Ceremony and provide guidance in contextual ministry methods to the staff at the mission. I have served as a consultant and interim staff member for the General Board of Global Ministries of the United Methodist Church's Office of Native American and Indigenous Ministries. I am a board member with NAIITS, the North American Institute for Indigenous Theological Studies: An Indigenous Learning Community, and a contributing writer for its academic journal and workshop presenter at its symposiums. I have ministered with Wiconi International for sixteen years, where I am working with Wiconi staff and colleagues to help take the organization through transitions and changes into its future.

Prior to the Wiconi director position, I made my living as a carpenter and worked for a general contractor for ten years in Albuquerque. All my life experiences have prepared me for the work I am currently doing. But before this life change in ministry I was a 'weekend warrior', as I like to call it, where I held a full-time carpentry position and was also involved in ministry on the weekends. I resigned my secular job as a carpenter, and I now work for the Master carpenter, Jesus Christ.

Journey in Contextual Ministry

In 1992 I had an experience so powerful that it divided my life into 'before and after'. While completing an English assignment in college, I wrote about my struggle to understand the separation of spiritual worlds in my life. What I was experiencing was the beginning of what I learned later was called 'contextual ministry'. As it turned out, I was ambushed: The combination of the class assignment and direction from the Holy Spirit revealed to me that there *is* a way to be fully Native *and* fully Christian. This all happened in a God-ordained dream/vision which I had dreamt and also seen while awake. I sensed the Holy Spirit was telling me not to disregard this revelation, but to listen, think about what I had just seen, consider the implications, and let my heart be 'grabbed' by the reality of the moment.

A Powerful Call from God

In my dream/vision I watched the unfolding story of a young boy embarking on his vision quest. He began with his father taking them on a four-day-walk, ending on the shores of Lake Michigan. He had fasted in preparation for this experience and grew physically weak but became more sensitive to the Holy Spirit's guidance. Upon their arrival at the shore, he and his father made a fire and built a shelter where they would wait for evening, hoping that when the boy slept, he might be granted a dream. While staring into the flickering colors of the fire, he fell into a trance and was taken away to a faraway land where he appeared in the midst of a group of people speaking a foreign language. They were wearing clothing made of fabric not seen in his land, and the men had much hair on their faces. Everyone was staring toward a hill where three poles were holding up three men. The men were all beaten and bloody, but the man in the middle was beaten far worse than the others, and there were thorns on his head.

The boy was confused about what he was seeing. As he took everything in, his eyes made contact with the man hanging on the middle pole. At that moment, each stared deeply into the other's soul, and the boy instantly understood why this man was there. With this revelation, he was swept back to the shores of Lake Michigan and found himself in the shelter with his father holding him tightly so he would not fall into the fire.

As the boy came to himself, he rested while his father roasted a rabbit over the fire and filled a wooden bowl of water for him to drink. When the boy was ready to share his experience, he asked his father if he could perform a ritual revealed to him in the vision. His father agreed and the boy, knowing nothing of Western Christian tradition, took a piece of the rabbit and the bowl of water and raised it to the twilight sky saying, 'As I eat this flesh and drink this water I do this to remember what the man on the middle pole was doing for us'.

Many more details were given to me in this dream/vision, but in my tradition, we are taught that you do not share the entire experience because doing so gives your vision away. The remainder of my dream/vision did much to enlighten my understanding of contextual ministry.

This revelation led my wife and me to begin our journey into contextual ministry by starting a church plant in Grand Rapids, Michigan, in the mid-1990s. This church plant began with two Anglo men who ran an after-school mentoring program for elementary and middle school students. One of these men was a former missionary to Muslims and a teacher at Cornerstone University in Grand Rapids. The other was a music major there. Their program was growing, and even some adult family members became involved. These two men sensed God's leading to expand this program into a Christian ministry outreach. Eventually they asked me to pastor this ministry, and as a result of our efforts it turned into a successful church plant. This new church was unique in that I was being led by God during this time to begin incorporating Native traditional rituals and ceremonies as authentic expressions of Christian worship and prayer. What resulted was the creation of one of the first contextual ministries in the country. The ministry met in a rented facility on Tuesday evenings and had an average attendance of fifty people.

Because of my use of cultural practices, the local churches in the area began to pay attention; some were supportive, some not so supportive, and some were totally against the initiative. With the help of several ministry friends and relatives, we discussed what was taking place in the ministry. They affirmed that what we were doing was right in the eyes of God and needed to be done. When we opened the doors for the first service, significant changes in the traditional approach to church planting had already been made. Among the cultural expressions incorporated were the Native drum as a musical instrument and arranging the worship area with chairs in a circle. I dressed in a Native-style ribbon shirt and sat down Native-style as I preached. The church service was opened with the burning of incense – this we call 'smudging', which is the fanning of the smoke of smoldering sage.

Beyond these practices, I would conduct other church-related services – such as funerals, weddings, and taking Communion – with the use of the sacred Native Pipe Ceremony. This is a ritual used by respected individuals in a community who are considered spiritual leaders or shamans. The Pipe Ceremony is conducted by joining a pipe bowl and a pipe stem together and (in my case) tobacco is placed in the bowl of the pipe and represents the prayers of the participants. The tobacco is burned and the smoke sent into the sky as a symbol of the prayers ascending to heaven. As I mentioned above, about fifty people came to our services. We did not know it at the time, but we were on the high end of attendance for most Native ministries in the country. Through this church plant, I learned that God was pleased with our ministry approach and the methods used as expressions of our Christian faith.

I felt God leading me to take another step and to incorporate the Native Sweat Lodge Ceremony. The sweat lodge in the Native world is a place of prayer where rocks are heated in a fire and placed on the ground in the center of a dome-shaped lodge. Water is then poured on the hot rocks to create steam so there is a cleansing of the participants both spiritually and physically.

The next step in our contextual journey was to include Powwow dancing as a natural part of our Native Christian world. Powwow is a form of social dancing which takes place most times in an outdoor arena where people gather for social or for competitive reasons – where dancers trained in various dance styles compete against each other for prizes. Dancing at the Powwows was a natural part of being a Native person in our community. Dancing was an acceptable social and spiritual practice and was enjoyed by many. Through it all, we felt a closer relationship with our creator Jesus Christ. Some consider Powwow dancing unacceptable for Christian participation. One time a person opposed to dancing asked me, 'What is the meaning of the Round Dance?' Now the Round Dance in my Native world is a social event where all in attendance can participate. In some cases, the Round Dance is a fine place for families to meet for potlucks and fellowship and also an excellent place for young adults to meet other young adults. My response to the Round Dance question was, 'I will tell you the meaning of the Round Dance when you tell me the meaning of the square dance!'

My Encounter with Richard Twiss

My spiritual growth during the time of the contextual church plant took me to places I never dreamed I would go. After we had been conducting services for about a year, I received a phone call from a cousin who told me with much excitement to turn on my television to the Trinity Broadcasting Network. I was astonished to see a man in full Plains Indian regalia with a headdress being interviewed on camera. I watched and listened with curiosity as he shared his message, and I realized it was the *same* message I was sharing about the need to create a new approach to Native ministry.

This was the first time I had heard of Richard Twiss. Up to this time we thought we were the only ones attempting this type of ministry experiment. Now this television program had piqued my curiosity, and I made plans to call him the following week. I took down the information from the program, and later I called the Wiconi International office in Vancouver, Washington. When Richard Twiss answered, I said, 'This is Casey Church of Grand Rapids, Michigan, and I caught your interview the other night'. The first thing he said to me was, 'We have heard all about you and your work in Grand Rapids, and I want you to know you're not alone'. We shared for a time in friendly conversation. This was my first meeting (albeit by telephone!) with another person outside our group who was speaking the same ministry language.

With this first conversation, we started a relationship that could only have been made in heaven. I became more involved with his ministry and was asked to join him and some others in an event called the Many Nations One Voice conference, known as MN1V. With this sequence of events, my ministry world was opened up to several of the main leaders in this new contextual movement – people such as Terry LeBlanc (Mi'kmaq/Acadian) and Randy Woodley (Keetoowah Cherokee). Many of us like-minded ministry leaders soon became a close ministry family.

Richard planned to host a camp in Oregon so he and others could create an environment where families could experience a Christianity expressed from within the Native American cultural and world view. My family and I did not attend this first event because we were involved in relocating to Albuquerque in 2000. After getting settled into our new home and community, we once again became more involved in the Wiconi ministry.

We were asked to come to Wiconi International's Family Camp in 2004 as part of the support staff. We were invited because of our knowledge of Native culture and traditions – and because our family celebrates life contextually. Wiconi was looking for partners they could trust with their innovative style of ministry. Many Native American outreaches were then getting more and more involved in contextualization. Several of them sprang up fast and wanted to join in as soon as they could – they wanted to get on the 'bandwagon' and ride on the popularity of Richard Twiss and all the attention the Wiconi organization was getting. Many wanted to join for the wrong reasons, and some were very eager but not fully ready theologically.

During the 2004 Family Camp, Lora and I sat in a gazebo just outside the main auditorium with Richard and Katherine Twiss. We told them we were feeling drawn by the Holy Spirit and would like to partner with them more fully than we had been. Richard and Katherine were honored to have us join them, and as I look back I know Richard was preparing us for a bigger role than just Family Camp. He had bigger plans to create an organization that would be a lighthouse to many Native American ministries and communities. To do this he was also nurturing others like us along the way.

My contextual leadership style and strength grew more as I was asked by Richard to be a board member with the North American Institute for Indigenous Theological Studies (NAIITS). At this time, Richard was the chairman of NAIITS. I also became more involved in the planning and implementation of contextual practices at Wiconi Family Camp. At the camp, I was given the responsibility to build – and *teach* the building of – the sweat lodge. They knew I had experience conducting Sweat Lodge Ceremonies contextually in Albuquerque. I also worked with the setup and coordination of the Powwow, which took place on Saturday. These responsibilities helped me to grow in knowledge of Wiconi Family Camp and in the ability to take on tasks within my comfort zone. All this made me more visible among the staff and volunteers at the camp, and soon I was able to manage many jobs there.

In the midst of everyday activity in ministry, I also grew in the understanding of who we were and how I could best serve within the Wiconi organization. Serving God in Wiconi under Richard Twiss' leadership was one of the most precious times of my life. Our efforts have not gone unnoticed, because whether I knew it or not, some people began to notice something in me that I did not know was even there. Although I sought to do the best possible job in every task I was asked to do, I always submitted to the leadership of Richard and the Wiconi staff. Contextual ministry was in my makeup, and I seemed to grow more and more in my capabilities at Family Camp, with the Brethren in Christ Mission, and everywhere I focused my ministry efforts.

After completing my Masters in Intercultural Studies at Fuller Theological Seminary, California, I still had the desire to continue my studies. In 2007 I applied for and was accepted to Fuller's School of World Mission (now School of Intercultural Studies) for a PhD in Intercultural Studies. I wanted to focus my studies in this program on the ceremonies used by the Hebrew and Native American people and look at the comparison between the two as they related to the use of incense and rituals. I also became interested in how the Hebrew people adapted various practices from the surrounding pagan culture's influences, and seeing how this might influence my work with Native American people. I chose 'Holy Smoke' as the working title for my study.

Retraditionalizing Rituals and Ceremonies

After a couple of classes, the tide of economic change was taking place across the country and it did not look bright. I had been providing for my growing family by working as a carpenter and tent maker for over a decade. In the spring of 2008 the economy fell and my employer had to lay off twenty-four of my fellow workers and me. As a result I made the choice to withdraw from the Fuller PhD program.

Economic times across the country got worse, and any type of employment was hard to find. We became typical of a family meeting the challenges of making it through this very hard time. Lora and I managed to keep the house, place food on the table, and clothe our five children. Times eventually got better. All through this I remained as active as possible in ministry at the Brethren in Christ Mission and with Wiconi Family Camp. During this time, Lora and I were not able to help with the cost of attending the camp, having put all of our resources into sustaining our home and family. Because of Richard's desire to have us maintain a presence at the camp and to stay involved, Wiconi made it financially possible for us to attend for several years. With the economy shifting to better times, we maintained our relationship with Richard and the Wiconi Family Camp.

It was during this time I felt I could return to my studies at Fuller and still maintain our family and home. I was accepted again and continued studying rituals in Hebrew and Native cultures, but included an additional focus on the Brethren in Christ Alcohol Treatment Program and the changes in the men as they went through the program and remained alcohol-free.

More Changes Ahead

When Richard Twiss suddenly passed on in February 2013, I volunteered to work at Wiconi Family Camp that summer. I had ten years of experience in leadership there and did not want it to be cancelled. The Wiconi board agreed, and I became the Wiconi Family Camp director. The next year I was asked to think about stepping up even more in leadership in the Wiconi ministry, and I took on some of the speaking engagements for which Richard would have been responsible. After that Family Camp, I was asked by the Wiconi board to come on as staff. This meant not only being the Family Camp director, but fulfilling several other commitments Wiconi had made before Richard's passing. One of these commitments included teaching at the Sioux Falls Seminary's Immersion Course held each July on the Rosebud Indian Reservation in South Dakota. And then another major change began to unfold in my ministry.

In January of 2015 I was asked to come to Vancouver, Washington, to meet with the Wiconi board, and they offered me the position of Director of Wiconi International. By this time, Lora and I had brought our family life and household to a very stable place – and now I was met with a decision to step into a position of an uncertain future with Wiconi, an organization going through great change and transition. I accepted the offer and the world of Casey Church was yet to experience more changes and periods of transition.

2

CAN WE IMPROVE THE WAY NATIVE MINISTRY IS DONE?

I know from personal experience as a Native American that all too often the Christian message and subsequent discipleship training have come to Native people with the non-Native Christian workers' cultural baggage attached. While spiritual transformation is the *ultimate* goal of presenting Christ's message, often it has been rejected as the 'White Man's Gospel'.

Background of the Study

My focus in writing this was initially to examine how the use of traditional rituals during recovery from drugs and alcohol has promoted a healthy Native American identity and helped Native people in recovery grow into a deeper relationship with Christ. I looked at two contextual ministries: The Brethren in Christ Overcomers (BICO) Alcohol Treatment Program and Wiconi International. As noted in Chapter 1, Wiconi International's annual 'Family Camp/Richard Twiss Memorial Powwow' encourages Native Americans and other Indigenous people to open their eyes so they can see how their own cultural forms have new meaning, thus helping them become stronger Christians.

After examining the use of contextualized rituals and their influence on spiritual growth, I turned to an exploration of the theme of Rites of Passage and its practical outworking in the

Overcomers program, the Wiconi Family Camp, and in leadership transition.

Brethren in Christ Overcomers Alcohol Treatment Program

In the desert Southwest there is a Christ-centered ministry called the Overcomers, which is a residential Alcohol Treatment Program for Native men operated by the Brethren in Christ Mission in Farmington, New Mexico. They have experienced a remarkable recovery rate of 70% or better. Since I first studied this program – which has been in operation since 1997 – they have had about one hundred seventy-five men participating. The curriculum is unique in that it incorporates the use of Native American prayer rituals and ceremonies in contextualized forms in a Christ-centered way. Additionally significant is that this ministry is staffed and run entirely by non-Natives. The Brethren in Christ Mission has earned good community relations with Native American people of the area by providing several amenities such as a laundromat, automotive service, and a well, so those on the reservation can have access to clean drinking water. For many of the Natives who are artists, the Mission provides a gift shop where they can sell their crafts or put them on consignment. Along with these services, the mission has a Sunday worship service where the local Native people attend fully contextualized church services and seasonal holiday activities.

I have been involved with this program for the past thirteen years by incorporating my knowledge of the Sweat Lodge Ceremony and other Native American rituals into this approach to alcohol treatment in a Christ-honoring manner. Overcomers has discovered that integrating this culturally-sensitive approach to ministry with Christian discipleship has led to an effective treatment program. Overcomers provides relational aftercare and support to ensure that the men remain alcohol-free. Staff rely on God's help throughout the process.

My goal was to explore the factors that have led to Overcomers' overwhelming success with Native American men's continued sobriety and Christian spiritual development.

The rituals and ceremonies we have incorporated into Over-comers are taken from the Native American traditional world of which I am a part. Through my ministry experience with Native American people and with Wiconi International, I have worked with others to develop acceptable Christianized Native rituals and ceremonies to be used in the Overcomers Alcohol Treatment Program. The incorporation of these traditional rituals into a Christ-centered scenario has created a model that can be adapted by other programs seeking to learn more about how to treat ad-dictions more effectively, and to encourage the spiritual develop-ment of the clients, and their ability to transition from addicts to productive community members.

Wiconi Family Camp/Richard Twiss Memorial Powwow Ministry

Wiconi Family Camp/Powwow is one part of the larger ministry events hosted by Wiconi International. Co-founded in Vancouver, Washington, in 1997 by Dr Richard Twiss (Sicangu Lakota) and his wife, Katherine, Wiconi aims to empower Native Americans by using traditional forms to encourage pride in their heritage and growth as Christians. It also teaches that they *do not* have to reject their cultural backgrounds in order to follow Christ.

After Dr Twiss' sudden passing in February 2013, the ministry plunged into a time of grief and confusion. Soon after, I was of-fered the role of Wiconi Family Camp/Powwow director. I was faced with the responsibility and opportunity to lead Family Camp without Richard during this turbulent time of transition. That year would prove to be quite a challenge for the staff and volunteers, but we worked together and became a team.

Richard Twiss often said Wiconi's mission was to bring about a 'preferred future' for our Native American people. As a result of his desire to see this vision fulfilled, he helped bring about a con-textual movement among many Native ministries across the coun-try and around the world. In order to accomplish this, Richard, like many others, was inspired to reexamine the evangelistic ap-proaches used to minister to the Indigenous people of North America. He wanted to see them introduced to the gospel of

Christ in a manner that retained their cultural identity and allowed them to be complete followers of Jesus. For too many years, Native people were required to deny their cultural identity and take on the cultures of foreign missionaries. Wiconi set out to counteract this mindset by encouraging members of the Native church world to adopt culturally-appropriate ministry to Indigenous peoples – referred to as 'contextualization'. In contextualization, Indigenous peoples' cultural ways are viewed as appropriate expressions of worship and honor to our Lord Jesus Christ. As a result, Wiconi became a hub around which many Native ministries sought partnership both formally and informally. Richard soon became very well known, nationally and internationally.

Wiconi Family Camp was born out of his ministry approach. There have now been eleven Family Camp/Powwows, and they are currently held at Aldersgate Conference Center in Turner, Oregon, in late July each year. Camp begins on Thursday afternoon and ends at noon on Sunday. It is attended by Native and non-Native people from the local region, across the United States, Canada, and even overseas. My family and I were not part of the first Family Camp but became regular ministry presenters from that time forward as Richard was intrigued with the method I used in the construction of the sweat lodge and in the way I conducted the ceremony inside the lodge. Further, while Richard was attending an event in Albuquerque, New Mexico, at my home church, we held a Powwow in the sanctuary. He then asked my wife Lora and me to help with his Powwow at the next Family Camp. Over the years since we have been treated as respected leaders in Albuquerque and have had several opportunities to be head dancers at Powwows in Albuquerque and other communities across the country.

The central focus of my study was to examine the contextual approaches used by Wiconi Family Camp/Powwow (from now on referred to as 'Family Camp' or 'Wiconi Family Camp'). Wiconi's main objective has been to promote contextual awareness and the practical application of the many rituals and ceremonies practiced among many of the tribes of North America. Over the years, Wiconi staff have adapted many appropriate Native American traditional rituals and ceremonies in a Christ-honoring way for participation by Family Camp attendees. The attendees experience and learn to apply and adapt these approaches to bless their own families or ministries. The adaptation of these various rituals and ceremonies – and their relations to the spiritual development of the camp attendees – is what I refer to as 'Rites of Passage'.

Rites of Passage occur worldwide among the traditions of many Indigenous peoples – even within the European peoples. Some of the rituals and ceremonies Wiconi has developed as contextual authentic Christian expressions include the sweat lodge, the use of incense in prayer, dancing at the Powwow, singing with the traditional Powwow drum, and the smudging ritual. Among others, ceremonies that can be contextualized would include a baby's first laugh, puberty rites, becoming a dancer, becoming a young man, and leadership status changes.

The Overcomers ministry and Wiconi Family Camp provide opportunities to show the importance of ritual. They also highlight the journey of contextualizing the gospel during the Liminal Phase of Rites of Passage.

The Historical Context of Native American Ministry

The history of evangelism among Native North Americans dating from the early days of contact in the 1600s has been an example of the intrinsic forces within the human psyche. The need to reinforce the dominant people's view of biblical history has shown itself around the globe as Indigenous people were being subjugated by those more powerful. This is called 'ethnocentrism', which is defined as 'the belief in the superiority of one's own cultural group'.[1] If we know what ethnocentrism is and how it affects the way we are influenced by it both individually and within our social systems, we can begin to see how much our understanding of scripture is influenced by our cultural bias. Our cultural bias raises its ugly head even in the realm of religion. For example, when engaged in church planting, why do we, when establishing churches in Native America, transfer our *own* culture to these new churches?

---

[1] 'Ethnocentrism', *American Heritage Dictionary of the English Language* (Boston, MA: Houghton Mifflin, 2nd edn, 1985), p. 467.

Cross-cultural missionaries plant churches identical to those in their home countries. Sherwood Lingenfelter describes this condition as being 'culture bound', causing many obstacles to effective mission work.[2] Is it possible to present a truly transformed gospel if we are always limited to replicating our own cultural reflection of Christianity wherever we carry the message?

When working among Native Americans, I start with a new focus. Twiss wrote in his groundbreaking book, *One Church, Many Tribes*,

> This is a time of transition in ministry among Indigenous believers around the world – a time of exploration and sincere inquiring of the Lord for new perspectives and approaches to Native ministry. Around the globe among Indigenous Christians, cultural identity is surfacing as the key dynamic in this emerging new Native ministry paradigm and spiritual awakening.[3]

During this time of transition, many doors of hope have been opened – with the confidence that many Indigenous ministries and churches across North America and around the world will reach their people using forms with which they can identify. But there has been stiff opposition as many Native ministries – whether operated by Native or non-Native staff – are trapped in the paradigm of the 'rightness' of European ethnocentric ministerial practices.

I believe that transitions are natural and necessary to the creation of needed change in Native American organizations, ministries, and people suffering from alcohol or substance abuse. Nevertheless, the dark cloud of conformity hangs over us all the time. Lingenfelter states: 'The social and cultural systems a missionary creates among local Indigenous communities exert powerful pressure on new believers and churches to conform to habitual stand-

---

[2] Sherwood G. Lingenfelter, *Leading Cross-Culturally: Covenant Relationships for Effective Christian Leadership* (Grand Rapids, MI: Baker Publishing Group, 2008), p. 15.

[3] Richard Twiss, *One Church, Many Tribes: Following Jesus the Way God Made You* (Ventura, CA: Regal, 2000), p. 19.

ards, values and practices'.[4] This pressure has carried over into the present as we can see from the many constraints our modern churches face each week. 'Rather than worship or evangelism, a church can fall prey to thinking that its purpose is keeping up a tradition, holding a particular event, or maintaining a building. These are good activities but they do not make up our purpose.'[5]

Our Lord Jesus Christ gave this commission to His disciples: 'Therefore go and make disciples of all nations, baptizing them in the name of the Father and of the Son, and of the Holy Spirit, and teaching them to obey everything I have commanded you. And surely I am with you always, to the very end of the age' (Mt. 28.19). One day this scripture opened my eyes to an oversight in my own life. This scripture does not give us a mandatory *prescription* as to how to accomplish this commission. I believe this was done purposefully to give us the freedom to make our approaches culturally specific to each people group.

Once I devoted my life to serving God through ministry, I focused on cultural awareness and the freedom in Christ that we Native believers have to utilize our own Indigenous culture for His glory. Over the years, I discovered that many others also had this passion. It became very apparent to me, as a result of this study and subsequent conclusions, that what I sought early in my contextual ministry was to become more Christ-centered in my approach. Still, what I really needed to do in this next phase was to become more focused on discipleship and spiritual development than on cultural contextualization. As leaders in Native American ministries, we must help the contextual movement ministry cohort to center on their new identity in Christ, and help lead them through the process of commitment to Christ and to one another, enabling them to be the people of God on mission together.

My emphasis was to see all life situations – ministry at the Brethren in Christ Overcomers, the Wiconi International organization, and personal leadership development – as going through a natural process of change. To accomplish this I used Victor

---

[4] Sherwood G. Lingenfelter, *Transforming Culture: A Challenge for Christian Mission* (Grand Rapids, MI: Baker Books, 1998), p. 18.

[5] J.E. White and L. Ford, *Rethinking the Church: A Challenge to Creative Redesign in an Age of Transition* (Grand Rapids, MI: Baker Publishing Group, 2003), p. 31.

Turner's concepts of 'Rites of Passage' and 'liminality', in which people move from structure to anti-structure and back to structure again. The middle period, anti-structure, he calls 'liminality', a time when labels are stripped away and people can build a sense of community with each other not founded on structural distinctions like power or gender.

Transition, Change, and Liminality

We all realize the world is not the same as it was in biblical times. Change and transition are natural processes we live with. I have studied many changes throughout Christian history and acknowledge that every culture where the gospel was presented underwent the challenge of understanding its message from that particular culture's viewpoint. So, contextualization is as old as the gospel itself! It was the *vehicle* of contextualization that promoted the rapid spread of the gospel until it stalled as reformers settled on what they thought were the ultimate modes of Christian expression.

Today Indigenous people around the world are awakening to the freedom to adapt the gospel into their own cultural contexts. This is our ultimate challenge from Jesus Christ – it is not to use our cultural ways as *the end* in itself with the primary focus being contextualization – but to use it as the vehicle to allow us entry into Native people's worlds through their hearts and minds in order to present Jesus Christ in a manner more natural to them. Contextualization is not intended to be a passing trend or a cute or popular way to conduct ministry, but a much-needed and serious approach to overcome the ineffective methods we have used in the past, and in some cases continue to use. I previously focused too much effort on the development of contextual approaches. Now I seek to take those created cultural forms and concentrate on their use for making disciples and increasing spiritual development.

By using contextual approaches, I have grown in my personal spiritual life and in my trust in God – a journey which has been a challenge for me. This journey has been periodically interrupted by conservative leaders with accusations of 'syncretism', which is the combining of two religious beliefs in a way that corrupts both. Critical contextualization does not take the beliefs of a religious practice but rather the *cultural* forms of those practices and adapts them in a way that creates a new expression – one that does not compromise the gospel message but makes it more palatable to Indigenous people. There are many Native Christian leaders who firmly resist and oppose the efforts to create a world where Native Americans can express their Christian faith in a manner more closely tied to their world view and cultural practices. The insistence of the use of a Western biblical viewpoint makes no sense from a Native perspective and has no connection to culture – as if all Hebrew traditions were fully Western! In their view, authentic Christian expression as planted in the Native world must look, act, sound, and feel just like today's Western church models. Western church methods have had dismal results in Native evangelism, with fewer than 5% of Native Americans identifying as Christian. This is even after *450 years* of missionary efforts. Because of these unacceptable results, the BICO program chose to conduct their church services and treatment activities from a fully contextual approach. Since then, the Sunday service is conducted contextually, and many Native people attend. For the same reason, the treatment program is experiencing about a 70% success rate for Native men recovering from alcohol abuse and addiction. Overcomers is continuing to see lives changed as many of the men are accepting Christ as their personal Savior. With all of the opposition and resistance to change, my question is, 'Where are the successful Western-style churches and treatment programs effectively helping Native people?' The Brethren in Christ program statistics speak for themselves. Such positive results do not occur without change and transition, but as with any change, the process has a beginning, middle, and end. This process extends into all areas of life, even with those who oppose contextual changes. I have had experience with several individuals who were very much opposed to contextual methods, and then later, having investigated the issues more fully, finally ended up as supporters and even active participants in contextual ministry.

The Overcomers program itself highlights the change process. The men come to the program, which is an ending of one part of life as they knew it, and the beginning of a new. Three months into treatment is the middle time, where new ways of living are taught – this is the liminal period, a time when change can take place. Then comes the ending of the program and the beginning of a new way of life called 'reintegration'. This process is a natural Native traditional way and is an experience many Native people are familiar with in their personal family lives. This can be seen in, as stated earlier, puberty rites, community status changes, and rituals to become a man or a warrior. Bridges says, 'while the changes we are facing differ from any we've experienced before, the transition process by which people get through change is well mapped'.[6] Native people have historically developed rituals and ceremonies to cope with these changes and transitions within their own 'map'. I believe it is this understanding of the change and transition process I continue to use in my traditional life and family life that has helped to create successful contextual ministries.

What is change and how do we bring it about? By looking at the changes the clients at the Overcomers Alcohol Treatment Program undergo, we can see that they move from being trapped in the quagmire of drugs and alcohol addiction to an in-between time of relearning life from a Christian world view, and then stepping into the same world with a whole new life focus. This is exactly what happens in a Rite of Passage. In the same manner, ministries and organizations can move through such stages and emerge on the other side of change – ready to face the world. The point is to create changes that will impact a positive future.

Rick Richardson, in his book *Ministry Outside the Box,* says, 'Every ministry born in the 1960s or before probably needs significant and sometimes painful soul-searching and change, especially in the area of its sacred practices in order to thrive and be fruitful today'.[7] These words are full of disdain for ineffective forms that for too long have determined the only approaches to ministry around the world. This is an area I have always struggled with when working with ministries unsure of moving contextually. I have this image of the future when I will stand before my Lord and He asks

---

[6] William Bridges, *Managing Transitions: Making the Most of Change* (Boston, MA: Da Capo Press, 2009), p. x.

[7] Richardson, *Evangelism Outside the Box*, p. 23.

me if I did everything possible to make the message of His Son Jesus available to Native people. I want to be able to stand before God and say, 'Yes, I did everything possible'. The issue at hand is, are we doing all we can to disciple and advance the spiritual development of the lost? Dr Gilliland, in his work *Pauline Theology and Mission Practice,* says,

> The important point that underlies this is that Paul's churches were meeting the special needs of natural groupings of people and were communicating the gospel in relevant forms and in languages that were suitable to each group and place. Those churches of Paul's ministry were not foreign or strange. They were flexible, open fellowships deferring in style and form, yet committed to basic teaching and features of worship that identified them all as one.[8]

For this type of ministry to take hold and became a movement, Paul knew the necessity of the process of transition and change and used it fully.

For clients at Brethren in Christ, or organizations such as Wiconi International, and for leadership development to happen, there must be change and transition. The Christian church must realize that ineffective methods must be adapted to influence the world. This is not an easy task. Many mission-minded thinkers have had ideas as to how to make this happen. One of these innovators was Paul Hiebert, who acted on this challenge with his concept of critical contextualization. Looking at the Native American traditional world with critical eyes has reinvented the work of the BICO program. The leaders of the Overcomers created a new approach by adapting the Native American world view, seeing the world as a whole, and accepting the sacredness of all aspects of their ministry life.

The same has taken place in Wiconi International and the leadership role I have been given. But unfortunately, people often occupy themselves with doing business and management as usual so that little time or effort is taken to think *ahead* of the curve. Looking ahead is realizing that transition and change are part of life.

---

[8] Dean S. Gilliland, *Pauline Theology and Mission Practice* (Eugene, OR: Wipf and Stock Publishers, 1996), p. 210.

Within Native American lifeways, all life is sacred, that is, it is full of ritual and ceremony. In the contextual ministry realm, life becomes an experimental process wherein ceremonies are *developed* to bring about a desired end. In a world of transition and change,

> Framing everything as an experiment offers you more running room to try new strategies, to ask questions, to discover what's essential, what's expendable, and what innovations can work. In addition, an experimental form creates permission and therefore some protection when you fail.[9]

Is There Really a Problem?

In order to promote positive change, I began looking at the cultural forms used in each ministry. My aim was to investigate how the use of Native cultural forms in two contextual ministries (the BICO Alcohol Treatment Program and Wiconi Family Camp ministry) creates a liminal spiritual experience that leads to freedom in Christ and to deeper spiritual formation for the participants. I also wanted to discover and analyze how BICO and Wiconi staff members perceive the effectiveness of using Native cultural forms in their Christ-centered alcohol treatment and Family Camp programs. I had to discover and analyze how the participants perceive the approach used by the two programs as being effective in, respectively, setting them free from past addictions, and in spiritual formation in Christ for the attendees of Wiconi Family Camp. I looked at how Native prayer practices and rituals used as a component of BICO's overall approach to ministry for addiction recovery led to spiritual formation among the clients as does Wiconi Family Camp's contextual program among its attendees. I then compared how the staff and participants at each program responded to the use of biblical scripture and Christian beliefs in these ministries.

---

[9] Heifetz, Linsky, and Grashow, *The Practice of Adaptive Leadership*, p. 277.

3

HISTORICAL REVIEW OF TRANSITION AND CHANGE

The overarching theme of my work has been to examine how change and transition are handled by individuals and groups – especially within the Native American world – and with organizations and ministries working with Native American people. My specific focus has been on the phase of Liminality and the concept of Rites of Passage.

Victor Turner and the Ritual Process

Victor Turner, one of the foremost thinkers on transition and change and the ensuing implications, focuses on the in-between time called 'liminality' and also the relationship of community to the individual and society in his book, *The Ritual Process: Structure and Anti-Structure*. His description of the process of working through some of his own thoughts gave me a better understanding of the relational side of change and transition. Turner was not satisfied with the approach used by other researchers to study cultures, especially in the way rituals were analyzed. He saw that an outsider could not do an adequate job of interpreting the ceremonial practices of another culture. He was conscious of the way some who study cultures were implanting their own thoughts into the Indigenous person's explanation. To offset this problem, Turner chose to use the Indigenous format, which stresses the *inner* meaning of the ritual being studied.[1] Although the concept of 'Rites of Passage' is credited to Arnold van Gennep, Turner focused on the Liminal Phase of the transition period of initiation rites.

Arnold van Gennep defined 'Rites of Passage' as 'rites which accompany every change of place, state, social position, age, and most areas involving change and transition'.[2] Turner regards the transition as a process, a becoming, and in the case of 'Rites of Passage', even a transformation.[3] Turner defines the stages as Separation, Liminality, and Reintegration. These phases can be seen in the BICO Alcohol Treatment Program and in the organizational changes Wiconi International encountered after Richard's passing. They can also be applied to my own life situation as I transition into directing Wiconi as an organization. The schema detailed by van Gennep and others has shown that '*rites de passage* are not confined to culturally defined life-crises, but may accompany any change from one state to another'.[4] These could include such areas as relocation, conversion, loss of loved ones, recovery after a natural disaster, and in my study, transition out of addiction, organizational change, and passing of the leadership baton.

These various times of transition and change can be placed into what Turner calls rituals and ceremonies. Rituals have a closer association with a *social state*, which is where rituals are *transformative* and ceremonies are more *confirmatory*. Turner states, 'Even as the initiate in a tribal culture must relinquish former structural ties, undergoing nakedness, poverty, and complete submission to the terms of liminal passage in order to attain the next life stage, so the individual in our own culture must leave old ways behind, divesting oneself of ego's claims to rank and social function, in order to attain a more highly individuated stage of growth'.[5]

---

[1] Victor Turner, *The Ritual Process: Structure and Anti-Structure* (Piscataway, NJ: Transaction Publishers, Rutgers, 1969 reprinted 2008), p. 94.

[2] Turner, *The Ritual Process*, p. 94.

[3] Louise C. Mahdi, Steven Foster, and Meredith Little, *Betwixt & Between: Patterns of Masculine and Feminine Initiation* (Peru, IL: Open Court, 1987), p. 4.

[4] Mahdi and Little, *Betwixt & Between*, p. 5.

[5] Mahdi and Little, *Betwixt & Between*, pp. 3-6.

Liminal Studies in Christian Ministries

Alan Roxburgh writes,

> Rites of Passage are rituals, usually religious in nature, through which individuals are detached from their established and normal role in society by being placed outside the social nexus in an in-between state; and after some ritualized passage of time, they are returned, inwardly transformed and outwardly changed, to a new place and status.[6]

He shows how the Bible narrative is full of Rites of Passage stories involving beginnings and endings, in-between stages of liminality, and endings that occur before new beginnings can start. These cycles are evident in every book of the Bible, as are ceremony and ritual. Ceremony marks the beginning of an end, and liminality experiences in scripture often had these processes and results. Roxburgh describes how in the books of Hosea and Exodus, the desert is the place where the people of Israel entered the most profound spiritual reshaping experiences of their lives. It was in these liminal areas that the potential for a new future was forged. Examples of these are seen in the lives of the Hebrew people when they enter Egypt, spend time there, and then experience the Exodus. Then they once again go through the same process as they leave Egypt, spend time in the desert, and enter the Promised Land. The Hebrew people of the scriptures were tribal people, and many of their life situations are similar to those of Native Americans. 'As Native people, we are in between the worlds of yesterday and where we will be, between traditional world views and Western rationalism, between community and individuality, between spirituality and religion'.[7] These places are neither good nor bad, only a part of life, and they require time to learn from for they are primal states, familiar to all cultures in which new beginnings can emerge.

In *Transforming Culture,* Lingenfelter shows us that 'Transformation means a new hermeneutic, a redefinition, a reintegration of the lives of God's people'.[8] On the one hand, for transfor-

---

[6] Roxburgh, *The Missionary Congregation*, p. 24.
[7] Twiss, *One Church, Many Tribes*, p. 35.
[8] Lingenfelter, *Transforming Culture*, p. 19.

mation to take place, new methods, approaches, and ideas must be conceived and put into practice.

On the other hand, William Bridges says, 'When you're in transition, you find yourself coming back in new ways to old activities'.[9] These phases of growth are indispensable if change is to occur. The stages of separation, liminality, and reintegration begin. The liminal time is also called the 'neutral zone' by Bridges. 'The neutral zone is not just the meaningless waiting and confusion that it sometimes seems to be. It is a time when a reorientation and redefinition must take place, and people need to understand that'.[10] Liminality is necessary. It can be seen from two cultural standpoints. In both Western and Native American understanding, the liminal 'is a moment out of time and out of secular social structure, a limbo of status-less-ness. A liminal state is often seen as sacred, powerful, and holy and a set apart time in which the old structure, rules of order, and identities are suspended.'[11]

Ritual Process and Change

Contextual ministry methods are now being used widely throughout North America and in many areas around the globe. Changing times and mindsets have opened the door to allow approaches that incorporate Rites of Passage rituals. Through their use, Indigenous people are finding a wholeness and balance to their lives that has been missing.

People face crucial events in their lives that initiate transition and change. 'As individuals grow up within the family and reach critical stages of transition, members hold Rites of Passage for those individuals to initiate them into the new stage of structured relationship.'[12] Organizations, individuals, and churches – by using their *own* traditions – are beginning to find their God-given place in the body of Christ, thereby putting life into harmony with the world. The many Native nations across North America have such ceremonies to create this harmony – for example, the Navajo of

---

[9] Bridges, *Transitions: Making Sense of Life's Changes*, p. 7.
[10] Bridges, *Managing Transitions: Making the Most of Change*, p. 43.
[11] Hiebert and Shaw, *Understanding Folk Religion*, p. 297.
[12] Lingenfelter, *Transforming Culture*, p. 167.

the Southwest call this *Hozho*, 'being in harmony'. We can choose to resist or embrace change. Either way, there are consequences.

Many individuals, organizations, and ministries are not seeking change. They make no effort to discover methods to create new and better ministries, structures, or leadership styles. No, their mission is simply to maintain the status quo, which can (humorously) be called, 'the mess we're in'. It's like keeping an old car that needs to be put to rest, but instead we do minor fixes to keep it running. In many cases we only do the minimum – wash the windshield, check the fluids, and wax the outside – but this course of action remains ineffective. In the same way, some ministries and pastors would rather stick to the 'old ways' with poor results than make the needed changes that God would honor and favor if they would only trust Him. It should be clear that when an organization gets to a point where they know they are not doing *all they can* to advance the gospel of Christ, they need to step into a period of change and accept a 'Rite of Passage' phase in their ministries.

In his seminal work on leadership, Bill Hybels observes that there are starting points, mid-points, and ending points in ministry.[13] Bridges states that every ending starts a new beginning, middle, and ending, and that this continues over and over. But he says that *transition* is different: 'The starting point for dealing with transition is not the outcome, but the ending you'll have to make to leave the old situation behind'.[14] In order to accomplish this I've heard it said, 'You can't get to where you're going until you leave where you've been'. Dan Southerland in his book, *Transitioning: Leading Your Church Through Change,* says that transitioning to a new way of doing anything is always hampered by the attitude he called the 'Seven last words of a dying church: We never did it that way before', when dealing with ministries and organizations on the edge of failure.[15]

How does this relate to the BICO Alcohol Treatment Program and the use of Native traditional prayer practices in a Christian

---

[13] Bill Hybels, *Courageous Leadership: Field-Tested Strategy for the 360° Leader* (Grand Rapids, MI: Zondervan, 2009), p. 43.

[14] Bridges, *Managing Transitions: Making the Most of Change*, p. 7.

[15] Dan Southerland, *Transitioning: Leading Your Church Through Change* (Grand Rapids, MI: Zondervan, 2002), p. 23.

ministry? At the Overcomers program, Native American traditional prayer practices are used as a natural part of the treatment.
It is of utmost importance that these Indigenous expressions of
Christian faith be firmly rooted in light of scripture and the historical living Christ. Paul Hiebert asks how Christians should re-
spond as new converts honor their past cultural practices: 'How
far can the gospel be adapted to fit into the culture without losing
its essential message, and who should decide?'[16] I have found these
questions to be very relevant when reflecting on the change and
transition I've encountered over the past two decades, including
my entry into leadership with Wiconi. Dancing on the edge of
authority is a scary place to be; either when considering the authority of scripture, or the formal or informal authority granted by an
organization. The challenge is further complicated because the
boundaries are not fixed in stone. The only way you know that
you are dancing on the edge of your scope of authority is by the
degree of resistance you encounter when you make a move.[17]

Resistance can come from several directions. There are those
who want to maintain the power, those who oppose any new approach to ministry, and those who are overly cautious about moving in any direction other than the familiar. In the contextual ministry approach, I agree with the following: 'Where clear biblical
principles contradict cultural values, the Bible takes precedence,
but where the Bible leaves room for flexibility, the cultural values
of the local host culture should normally prevail'.[18]

---

[16] Hiebert and Shaw, *Understanding Folk Religion*, p. 183.

[17] Heifetz, Linsky, and Grashow, *The Practice of Adaptive Leadership*, p. 283.

[18] James E. Plueddemann, *Leading Across Cultures: Effective Ministry and Mission in the Global Church* (Downers Grove, IL: InterVarsity Press, 2009), p. 89.

4

THE OVERCOMERS: THE BRETHREN IN CHRIST ALCOHOL TREATMENT PROGRAM

The Brethren in Christ Overcomers (BICO) Alcohol Treatment Program currently uses contextual methods I helped design and integrate. The program began in 1997, and at that time was very similar to most alcohol treatment programs across the country. The program initially had minimal success. Duane Bristow became the director and was motivated to take the program in a new direction to increase effectiveness. We met in 2001 at a leadership conference held by the Nazarene Indian Bible College in Albuquerque. From then on, we worked together to develop the program we have today, which now has a highly successful recovery rate of men leaving alcohol addiction – (between 70% and 75%) – a rate higher than seen in most programs. But it did not come easily; it took courage and the willingness to take risks to create a better future for the clients.

Many of BICO's original approaches from 1997 have been retained, including home living coordinators and Bible study materials. Each session maintains a low number of clients, ranging from six to eight, which encourages closer relationships between the staff and clients. Most of the coordinators are volunteers from Brethren in Christ churches from Pennsylvania, including two couples who, as their main ministry focus, model a Christian lifestyle for the clients. The program director attributes much of their success to the deep-level relationship building of these couples.

At my suggestion, new methods derived from a Native American point of view have been integrated. Family support is important, so the clients have the opportunity to visit with their families on Sundays. Development of the Christian faith is also vital. The use of contextualized rituals such as the Sweat Lodge Ceremony allow the men to pray in their own traditional, Indigenous way. For some, prayers are offered while burning incense – sage, sweet grass, cedar, or tobacco – held in an abalone shell. Another way to create a positive cultural identity has been the use of the Bible translated into Navajo. One other method that requires some risk-taking is the use of the Native drum on which the clients learn Christian songs. I have participated as the cultural advisor providing Christ-honoring Native rituals – a contextual approach that results in the development of a positive Native Christian identity.

Any type of change involves taking risks, and risk-taking goes against the grain of many denominational traditions. History has shown that the approaches used to evangelize many Native peoples around the world have used a Western ethnocentric model which denied local cultural expressions as acceptable to an Indigenous Christian faith. These methods continue and attempt to make other cultures into replicas of the sending church. Richard Twiss wisely said in his book *One Church Many Tribes*, 'Jesus does not ask us to abandon our sin-stained culture in order to embrace someone else's sin-stained culture'.[1]

Why Is BICO Different than Most Western-style Missions?

Many of the innovations implemented by BICO are cultural. When I first became involved with the Overcomers, the director and I met to discuss the need to make cultural changes in our approaches to Native ministry. I was then invited to work with them. This amiable relationship opened the door to experimentation in ministry methods. Of crucial importance was the inclusion of the topic of contextualization in our conversation – something that was not previously permitted. That permitted us to discuss what

---

[1] Twiss, *One Church, Many Tribes*, p. 79.

could or should not be allowed as acceptable adaptations. We decided to include worship methods identifiable to Native cultures, such as sitting in a circle while at the Sunday church service, as most Native meetings are conducted, thereby allowing the minister to sit instead of stand at the pulpit. We further initiated the use of incense in rituals such as blessing and prayer ceremonies. The use of incense in worship is not new for church services. The Catholic and Orthodox traditions have used it for years.

One last item incorporated into our Sunday church service was the use of the drum as our primary musical instrument. We sing and worship using a playlist of new songs composed for this style of worship, which incorporates other Native instruments and songs with Christian lyrics. The songs are easy to learn, especially for the Native men, because the Native musical style is familiar to them. Over the years, I have learned that there is no one exclusive musical style for Christian songs – there are only Christian lyrics.

The Overcomers program took an additional leap of faith and incorporated the use of the Sweat Lodge Ceremony. The sweat lodge is a traditional place for prayer, cleansing, and teaching. The lodge is not some 'spooky pagan ritual' but is an acceptable ceremony in this Christ-centered program. It is similar to a sauna found at any health club, and is constructed of mostly natural materials and then heated with rocks from an open fire. The sweat lodge is inherently used for physical cleansing but goes beyond that to help reverse the mental, spiritual, and emotional damage caused by life events. Many Native cultures use the sweat lodge, and each has its own traditional way of conducting it. Ours is conducted only by believers in Christ.

Since 1997, the program has served about 150 Native men. Over the years, some of the clients have become part-time volunteers. There is currently an active search for a facility near Farmington, New Mexico, to be used as a half-way house. If found and developed into the program, the staff believes the results will be even better.

BICO Research and Analysis

I wanted accurate knowledge of how the Brethren in Christ Overcomers staff members perceive the effectiveness of using Native cultural forms in their Christ-centered alcohol treatment program, so I interviewed both staff and clients and I became an active participant in Sweat Lodge Ceremonies and the contextual church services.

I have been involved with the BICO program for thirteen years. During this time, we created an approach to ministry unlike any other by incorporating Native cultural rituals and ceremonies into praise and worship and sermon time. As friendships with the staff deepened, I realized I wanted to conduct a detailed study (as a colleague) of the reasons for the program's outstanding success in recovering men from alcohol addiction. It is my hope that many others will be helped by learning the techniques used in the BICO Alcohol Treatment Program.

Selection of Clients for the Program

The program directors interview potential clients months before a program session begins. Once selected, arrangements are made to quickly enroll them and seek scholarships for their stay if needed. No one is ever denied for lack of funds. The men come from various prisons and jails. Some are court-ordered to attend a treatment program of their choice, but others request enrollment in the program.

At the beginning of each three-month session, I talk with the director and schedule three days when I will travel to the mission to conduct a Sweat Lodge Ceremony in a Christ-honoring way and teach about Native culture. The sweat has become a permanent part of the Overcomers approach to treatment, and it takes place on Saturday evenings once per month during the program. There are usually six to eight clients, two staff members, me, and on occasion a couple of visitors who attend.

The lodge is set up and a fire started to heat the rocks which will be placed inside. When I arrive, the staff gathers the clients and those attending. During the ceremony we use the Native Drum to accompany contextual worship songs they have been practicing. After the singing, I prepare the pipe for a Pipe Ceremony, also done in a Christ-honoring way. When this ritual is completed, we prepare to enter the lodge. I should explain that Native ceremonies and rituals start when we are ready and end when we are finished. The Sweat Lodge Ceremony lasts for sixty to ninety minutes. It has become a basic part of the program and is a safe place for the clients to share openly the struggles they have with alcohol and addiction. After the ceremony's conclusion, we go back to the treatment center, prepare a group meal, and get better acquainted with one other.

While at the Brethren in Christ Mission church service, I was a participant-observer – sometimes the speaker and at other times a visitor. The church service is held in the mission's gymnasium, which has a sound system and a stage. Instead of pews facing forward, we sit Native-style in a large circle. During the service, which takes place on Sunday afternoons, we begin with songs sung with the Native drum. We do not use an organ or piano, only the drum. Our drum is handmade, about twelve inches tall and thirty-six inches across. It is made of wood, and its drum surface is made of elk hide stretched and tied tightly. We beat the rhythm with handmade drum sticks. Sitting in a circle around the drum, which is situated just off center in front of the stage, we begin to sing the opening songs. Approximately twenty-five Navajo community members and fifteen staff and visitors attend the services. The mission director delivers the message sitting on a swivel chair with a music stand as his pulpit. An offering is taken during a drum song, and the attendees stand and walk forward to place their gifts on a Native-style blanket placed in the middle of the circle. Following the service, everyone stays for a potluck.

From this first analysis, I concluded that contextual methods are very important for the client's recovery if they are to develop a more positive self-identity and increase their self-esteem. At the time, I was narrowly looking for what I wanted to find. My ministry was then mostly focused on presenting 'how to do' contextual methods and approaches, and my work at the Overcomers was my laboratory. However, it is important to convey the fact that reintegration of ritual in itself does not produce significant improvement in the recovery rate – Jesus does.

As I examined the responses of the staff, home living coordinators, and denominational leaders in the analysis, my understanding of the data took on a whole new meaning. My re-analysis reflected a more balanced and objective approach to my interview data. In this second analysis, I did not change my questionnaire or the responses I received from the staff and the clients. The data I collected in the first analysis was still useful for this re-analysis. The only difference is in the way I went about coding and analyzing responses the second time. The new categories for analysis emerged from my less-biased analysis of the same data.

My re-analysis revealed very different findings from my first analysis. I observed many of the same contextual methods, but the data also indicated many other significant factors in the program's success. These additional factors included 'Life Skills' training, Christian Bible study, and relationship-building among the clients, staff, and home living coordinators. The more I looked, the more pronounced the differences. For example, one home living coordinator said that a sense of healing was as necessary as relationships and life skills training. When I allowed myself to look beyond contextual methods, I was able to see the other factors. I concluded that the success of the clients remaining drug and alcohol free after attending the BICO Alcohol Treatment Program was due to the program's Christian approach and the Christian relationships formed while participating. Many of the clients who responded also highlighted the importance of family and faith development.

One client mentioned that the use of prayer in the Native way has helped him grow closer in his faith in Christ. Many of those responding stressed the importance of classes in computer usage, financial management, the program's focus on Christian beliefs and values as applied to a Native Christian identity, and Bible study.

One client stated, 'I always spent my check on booze. Setting up a plan within the finance class was a real eye-opener for me to help me handle my money'. About half of the clients testified to the power of Christian relationships building, life skills training, and a sense of healing. One man stated, 'A life *with* Christ and *without* alcohol is what I really want. I am tired of my former way of life, and I pray I can stay sober after this program'. Another client said, as many do, 'I am sick and tired of being sick and tired'. I clearly saw that the modeling of Christian relationships and Christian lifestyles was critically important in achieving high recovery rates. It was this realization that made me push harder to see deeper into the data.

These findings were further confirmed by the group interviews with the clients. The interviews were much more practical because of the low educational level of many of the clients. Some of them were not able to read or express themselves in writing. When I sat down with them in a comfortable area and began to chat, I was able to bring up the interview questions. I was surprised by their candor. Their responses confirmed many of the factors made evident by my re-analysis of the data. When I asked them if the contextual style we used was important to their recovery, some of those responding said, 'They were OK, but the other parts of the program seem to be more helpful'. The program's incorporation of contextual approaches was not the main factor – as my previous analysis attempt had seemingly shown – but the contextual approaches did add to the clients' overall positive view of their Native identity. A more positive view of being able to live as both Native and Christian caused some to experience growth in their spiritual formation because of the incorporation of contextual methods into their religious lives.

BICO Alcohol Treatment Program as a Rite of Passage

After my Fuller seminary cohort's course on Change Dynamics, I was struck with the concept of 'Rites of Passage'. The concept deals with the change and transition dynamics that take place in what is called the 'Liminal Phase'. With this in mind, I took another look at the responses to the same questionnaires. After reading more on the subject, I went through the responses in search of themes dealing with Rites of Passage, and those images related to separation, liminality, and reintegration.

I have concluded that one of the key factors in our clients' success in their recoveries from alcohol addiction stems from the fact that the BICO Alcohol Treatment Program is an extended Rite of Passage, a ceremonial time in which the clients enter and go through a journey of reflection. Then reintegration takes place upon their graduation from the program. I found that the three phases of Rites of Passage were evident in the program's structure. The director says, 'The interview process is the first phase to freedom from alcohol and to life change'. Other staff members mention that the three-month period of isolation from the world – required to complete the program – is essential for the changes to take place in their lives. Some staff members said, 'It takes thirty to forty days to change a habit, and our program uses ninety days'. I agree that three months seems to be necessary for effective treatment. All staff members said that new information can be incorporated, and learning can happen in this length of time. Change and transition – an internal sense that healing is taking place, and recognizing their own new identity – are indications of the clients' navigation through the Liminal Phase. Some of the clients said, 'At first the three months seem like a long time for a program, but as we move through the weeks, it all happens very fast and before we know it, it's over'.

The program's success is proven by the transition and change occurring in the clients. The staff clearly indicated that the Overcomers program is life-changing, not only for the clients, but also for them. The basic approach of the program is to have everyone enter the Liminal Phase ready to take risks and use sacred items within an acceptable cultural manner – a manner also acceptable to our Christian faith. The realization that Native rituals and ceremonies can be used in a positive Christ-honoring way is an added benefit to the clients. The staff have said that 'The Sweat Lodge Ceremony is one of the most helpful aspects of the program because it gives the men an opportunity to pray in their own way'. The educational portion of the program is also very important for recovery. With the new information (Bible and life-skill instruction) there is a perception of confidence, healing, and a new identity gained as a result of the program's culturally-sensitive methods. One significant reason this program is so successful is that the program's approach is completely accepted by the staff.

The need for taking risks has always *found* me – I've never sought it out. To accomplish the success rates achieved by the BI-CO program, we had to engage in some risk-taking and integrate a variety of new methods. We had to motivate and encourage the denominational leadership and the program staff to trust God and us to 'experiment' with some options. Our 'laboratory' would be the treatment center at the Brethren in Christ Mission. Our 'tools' would be the willingness to try anything with Holy Spirit's guidance. We made up much of the curriculum 'on the run'. The Liminal Phase we entered was our time to take risks – the kind of risks we hoped would change lives. 'When you really don't know what to do, all you can do is become an artist. The motive for creative leadership is not a matter of whimsy, it is a matter of survival, making the future work.'[2] Being an artist myself (a potter and a traditional cradleboard maker) has helped me to be creative and willing to improvise in areas of ministry.

Integration of Native Ritual and Ceremony

We adapted Native rituals to create 'new' approaches used in the BICO Mission and its Alcohol Treatment Program. The sacred rituals that we adapted into contextual ceremonies were the Sweat Lodge Ceremony, Singing with the Drum using Christ-honoring lyrics, and Praying with Incense.

As noted previously, the Overcomers program now uses the Sweat Lodge Ceremony as part of its regular approach. While in the lodge, the clients express heart-felt prayers. They say, 'Praying in the sweat comes naturally and I know God understands my heart'. Using these Indigenous rituals gives the clients a feeling of cleansing, both spiritually and physically. It is my conclusion that the clients find a stronger connection with God praying in the lodge with staff than when sitting in a room. There are times in the 'sweat' when some of the participants will shed tears because of their deep desire to break free from alcohol's grip.

Singing with the drum is a learning experience for the clients and has become a central part of the recovery process. They sing their worship to God using Christian lyrics. Every group of men enjoys singing what one client called the 'click, click song', because the song starts off with a light tap of the drum stick stem on the edge of the drum and then begins with the lyrics, 'Jesus is Lord'. During this song, each of the men is given a chance to lead by singing the lyrics, 'Jesus is Lord'.[3] I have found that the drum becomes critical in the recovery process because of the relationships the clients make with the staff and home living coordinators as

---

[2] Heifetz, Linsky, and Grashow, *The Practice of Adaptive Leadership*, p. 207.
[3] This song is by Jonathan Maracle of Broken Walls. www.brokenwalls.com.

they play the drum and sing together. Also, teaching the clients
how to pray using incense became an important learning experience for them. Instead of being criticized for their Indigenous
style of praying, they are encouraged because their ways can be
used in Christian worship and prayer. By sending their prayers up
in the smoke from smudging or from the pipe, there is a unique
connection between God and them that only an Indigenous person can understand. Through the use of these cultural items and
ceremonies, the clients experience a positive Native self-identity as
they grow spiritually in Christ.

The Brethren in Christ Mission was and is a unique place. It
contains many of the particulars of a Christ-centered recovery
program but also incorporates Native American cultural practices.
In order to achieve their high success rates using Native American
practices, they have had to make the adaptive journey through
many changes and transitions. By doing so they have had their
own hearts and minds changed. They were willing to challenge
and transform their longstanding habits and deeply-held beliefs.
Strongly-held beliefs are referred to as 'cultural prisons' by Lingenfelter. He says, 'We need to comprehend the dimensions of
our cultural prisons, and discovery comes from the biblical keys
that will allow us to unlock the chains of our own cultural habits
and the gates to our own cultural walls'.[4] Understanding that we
all have these 'cultural prisons' has helped me in my own ministry
journey. I had fruitful results while working in my church in Michigan – creating many unique expressions of Christian faith from
within the existing Native American culture there – and when
working with Wiconi International.

While serving with the Brethren in Christ program, I created
and used expressions *suited* to Navajo culture and tradition. Dr
Gilliland in *Paul's Theology of Mission* describes similar approaches
to mission work saying, 'The greatest gift a missionary or mission
agency can give to a young church is the right to think out and act
out the Christian life for itself'.[5] Working toward an expression
fitting of a truly Indigenous church is our goal. The staff and I
see our work as being a mediating work of Christ within the cli-

---

[4] Lingenfelter, *Transforming Culture*, pp. 19-20.
[5] Gilliland, *Pauline Theology and Mission Practice*, p. 221.

ents' own environment. But for *solid* change to continue to take place, innovations must become an integral part of the ministry's culture. This kind of courageous change soon reaches a point of no return – when the old ways of the 'cultural prison' no longer overpower the new ways.

The Brethren in Christ Mission has been bold enough to embrace needed changes, and these changes have overflowed into all areas of their ministry. The transition process has developed new and creative approaches as well, but these have come as a result of having an experimental mind-set. It is this mind-set that is promoting the spiritual development not seen in the older approaches of the treatment of alcohol addiction. It is a process that faces the clients' behavioral problems biblically and relationally using ritual and ceremony.

Understanding the processes of change and transition helps us as we analyze the older approaches used by other Christian alcohol treatment centers. By examining the former Western styles of treatment, which included their own rituals and ceremonies, we can understand how *culture-bound* they had become. Since they took their own cultural expressions of Christian faith to the world, it is no surprise then that Christianity was often seen as a foreign religion and Christian converts as 'aliens in their own land'. This is true in my ministry world in the Southwest, and it holds true in many other areas of the country. Many non-contextual churches maintain the foreign forms they have used in their ministries for years. This is true of the majority of reservation churches – they essentially continue to promote the ministry styles taught them by their denominations. The current generation of Native people finds little meaning in these Western ministry styles. But changes have continued to take place; our Native ministry has changed from culturally-restrictive to culturally-inclusive.

5

WICONI FAMILY CAMP/POWWOW

With the sudden death of Dr Richard Twiss, the president of Wiconi International on Feb. 9, 2013, my ministry world and studies at Fuller took on drastic changes. In addition to the information gathered at the Brethren in Christ Overcomers (BICO) Alcohol Treatment Program, I saw the opportunity to learn more by focusing the next phase of my research on the change process occurring among attendees of Wiconi Family Camp/Powwow and also on the changes the Wiconi International ministry was about to go through.

Wiconi International created a place (Family Camp), where a Christ-centered Native American contextual program can reach the hearts, minds, and spiritual needs of the people who gather there. The Wiconi Family Camp/Powwow (from now on referred to as Wiconi Family Camp or Family Camp) is more effective in reaching Native people at their heart-level than a Western-style mission outreach. The Powwow and Family Camp attract many Native people who live within a faith and culture conflict. At Family Camp we invite them to explore what a Christian life can be like as a Native American believer. They have the opportunity to enter into a new internal wholeness – which *includes* their cultural identity as Native Christians.

Richard Twiss related the story of a Cree woman who experienced this internal wholeness at Family Camp. She had lived doubting God's love for her because she was Native. After hearing Richard's teaching, she said that for the first time she now believed that God fully loved her and that she did not need to feel ashamed anymore.[1] Another camp attendee shared that he felt the Lord was giving back the Native cultural ways that the devil had stolen and tried to destroy. He now believes he is set free to be Native again.[2] These are examples of the transformed lives we have been seeing during Wiconi Family Camp events.

The Structure of Wiconi Family Camp

Wiconi Family Camp takes place in late July at Aldersgate Camp and Retreat Center in Turner, Oregon. Attendance at the camp varies from 250 to 300, mostly made up of Native families from the Pacific Northwest region. Native ministry leaders from across the country and interested people from various backgrounds also attend. Camp begins with registration at 4.00 pm on Thursday and runs until noon Sunday. The camp is structured around selected themes, some dealing with Native family and community issues, and some devoted to theological topics covering various aspects of ministry among Native American churches. For example, in 2014 the Family Camp theme was contextual Christian worship, where music-related topics were discussed and presentations made. Popular Native contextual Christian musicians were invited to participate, including Dr Cheryl Bear (Nadleh Whut'en First Nation), Jonathan Maracle (Mohawk), and Bill Pagaran (Tlingit) of Broken Walls.

The theme for 2015 was suicide prevention in Native communities. A video created by and for Native people called, 'Through the Pain',[3] was shown to the attendees. Notable First Nations and American Native pastors and counselors then facilitated serious but upbeat discussions and presentations about suicide prevention. Suicide rates on American Native reservations and Canadian First Nations reserves are extremely high.

Family Camp is pleasantly situated among the cedars and Douglas firs of the Pacific Northwest. There is also a beautiful stream where families enjoy tubing, wading, and meditation. The

---

[1] Twiss, *One Church, Many Tribes*, p. 163.
[2] Twiss, *One Church, Many Tribes*, pp. 161-63.
[3] This DVD may be purchased in the resources section at www.wiconi. com.

campers can choose from a variety of many other family-oriented events. Traditional craft-making activities are provided for both young and old. Classes have included bead work, copper bowl-making, and the construction of rattles and hand drums. Outdoor activities have included a water slide, rock-wall climbing, a ropes course, and volleyball. Wiconi chose Aldersgate because of its peaceful atmosphere and an arena large enough to hold a Native American Powwow. Our Powwow is a traditional event where individuals come dressed in their cultural regalia, and they can dance to the drumming of several drum groups from the region.

Over half the attendees are made up of Native families. Many are offered scholarships. Some of them would not be able to attend without financial assistance due to the lower economic level of many of the reservations in Washington and Oregon. We also offer scholarships to twenty-five young people and their youth group leaders. The camp is attended by many Native ministry leaders from a variety of denominations including Foursquare, Methodist, Baptist, and Assembly of God. Every year, about one third of the Camp attendees are there for the first time. On many occasions, we have Bible college students, missionaries, seminary professors, and missiologists attending the event.

Wiconi Family Camp Agenda

The usual agenda for Family Camp is as follows: Registration starting at 4.00 pm, dinner at 5.30 pm, followed by a gathering in the auditorium for worship led by an invited contextual musical group. Then there is time for fellowship. On Friday, we begin with breakfast together, gather for worship, and then have the first of the presentations until it's time for lunch. Children are dismissed to programs especially designed for them. The afternoon is slated for family craft time and other fun activities. After dinner, we gather for 'talent night' where individuals are invited to share their personal talents, such as singing, skits, dance routines, poetry, and rap songs. Saturday morning after breakfast we gather for another presentation, and then we prepare for the traditional Powwow, which lasts from noon until 10.00 pm. On Sunday morning, we wrap up the weekend with our final worship time and presentation. After that, the attendees say their farewells with hugs and tears.

Building the Sweat Lodge

One of the more traditional aspects of the camp is the construction of the sweat lodges. This is one of the first activities we start upon arrival at the campground. I take a group of interested people and assistants and build two sweat lodges. The sweat lodge is a dome-shaped structure covered with canvas and tarps to keep the heat inside. The heat for the sweat lodge is created by stones which have been in an open fire pit for several hours. They are brought into the lodge when the Sweat Lodge Ceremony is to take place. After the proper ceremonial protocol is completed, those participating enter the lodge and take their seat around the circle. A bucket of water is brought into the lodge and several dippers full of water are poured on the hot stones, creating steam which adds to the cleansing nature of this spiritual ceremony.

The ceremony is meant to bring about both spiritual *and* physical cleansing. The Sweat Lodge Ceremonies are conducted both morning and evening. (I will explain this ritual and others in greater depth in the next section). The sweat lodge is similar to a fitness club sauna, with both using heat and steam. Sweat lodge attendees experience not only a physical cleansing from the hot steam – they also have spiritual, mental, and emotional cleansing resulting from the prayers and open conversations in the lodge.

Family Camp Ministry Approach

The BICO Alcohol Treatment Program promotes freedom from alcohol and substance abuse in addition to spiritual formation in Christ. Wiconi Family Camp's ministry emphasizes family fun, Christian fellowship, and spiritual growth in Christ. Contextual spiritual practices are used in the camp ministry.

With people from a wide variety of backgrounds in attendance at Family Camp, our approach needs to be flexible enough to meet the many group and individual ministry needs. The main emphasis of Wiconi's approach is to 'look, smell, sound, feel, and taste Native'. Richard Twiss was able to create, with the help of many supporters and colleagues, a place (Family Camp) that reflected the culture and world view of Native people.

It is my intention to present a clearer understanding of the Native rituals and traditions we have adapted, using insights gained from the Native American Contextual Ministry Movement. A few of the Native cultural aspects emphasized during Family Camp are worship with Native music led by Native musicians, a worship center reflecting the Long House style of the Native people of the Pacific Northwest, instruction using a Native storytelling method, cultural teaching during craft time, and the traditional style of the main event – the Powwow. These represent only a few of the approaches we have introduced.

Richard Twiss wanted to keep the structural organization of Family Camp simple. The need for this type of gathering became apparent because of the success of a series of conferences called 'Many Nations, One Voice'. These were Wiconi-run and held in many cities across the nation. The conferences were highly-structured and focused on contextual ministry, philosophy, and methods. When these conferences were discontinued, Wiconi went in a new direction by creating Family Camp. The idea was to offer a camp where those working tirelessly in their respective regions could come together and share the stories of the battles they were facing to promote contextual ministry. With less structure than the conference series, Family Camp was to be a place to just have fun and build relationships with others working in contextual ministry. Those attending the camp became a very tightly-knit family, referring to each other as brothers and sisters, and uncles and aunties. These Family Camps are known for offering the attendees contextual Sweat Lodge Ceremonies where those new to the sweat lodge could experience them in a safe and Christ-centered atmosphere. The camp took the additional step of offering a traditional Native American Powwow, allowing attendees the opportunity to dress in their respective cultural regalia and dance as others do at traditional Powwows across the country.

A Living Laboratory of Contextual Ministry

Before describing the cultural innovations we used, we must remember that contextualization was not a very popular topic twenty years ago. The founding of Wiconi International caused contextualization to be looked at more seriously. Several Native American ministers and scholars started to have ideas of their own. When they began to attend Wiconi Family Camp, 'critical mass' was formed and the ride began!

Twiss' idea to expose leaders to models of contextual ministry methods at Wiconi Family Camp was nothing short of sheer genius. If a picture is worth a thousand words, then a *living* example is worth ten thousand words. Wiconi Family Camp was created to be the living laboratory where we break open the 'can of creativity' and make a Native American expression of Christian faith in a fully Native setting. We decided that the camp must be more than just some Native American evangelical copy looking like a thousand other Christian camps. Instead, we wanted to offer an innovative ministry event that effectively met the needs of Native people. Many of these innovative methods were created to include ethnic traditions that may have had negative connotations attached to them by pastors and missionaries who had not taken the time to understand them.

We selected several ceremonies and rituals common to many tribal traditions. A few of these sacred rituals and ceremonies include: the Sweat Lodge Ceremony, Praying Using Incense ('Smudging'), Powwow Dancing, Singing with the Hand and Big Drums, and playing the flute.

But first, a word of explanation is warranted. The following are not meant to be descriptions or explanations of the *traditional* uses of various rituals or ceremonies common to the belief systems of North American tribes, but *rather* rituals and ceremonies that have been 'retraditionalized' as contextual expressions of Christian faith. The forms and meanings are *my* re-interpretations of them both as a Native traditional and Christian practitioner. The descriptions will show how we can have the freedom to apply Christ-honoring meanings to old rituals and create functional expressions that can meet the spiritual needs of Native people – needs that were never met when presented with the gospel in the past.

As is attributed to St. Francis of Assisi, my approach is to be a 'living' gospel (to preach the gospel – and when necessary, use words). What I mean by this is: I *live* a Native American traditional lifestyle as a believer in Christ mostly by *example* instead of using words presented in sermons. I conduct the ceremonies and rituals without much in the way of interpretive commentary or explanation. But in order to share the gospel message more clearly to those who do not know their traditional heritage, I take time with the group and instruct them in the steps of the contextualized ritual I am performing – and I do not mean performing as 'performance'. I mean conducting the sacred ritual with commentary. I explain the following rituals as an attempt to give insight into the contextual ministry world, including my work at both the Brethren in Christ Mission and Overcomers Alcohol Treatment Program and with Wiconi Family Camp.

Construction of the Sweat Lodge: A Contextual Approach

Each year *upon arrival* at the Wiconi Family Camp, we begin the Sweat Lodge Ceremony. Some may think that the only aspects important to the ceremony take place in the lodge during the ritual itself. Not so, as the Sweat Lodge Ceremony begins with the building of the lodge and ends when it is taken down. For Native people, every part of life is sacred – that includes the process, not just the final objective. The various stages of the construction process are precise, beginning with the clearing of the ground where the lodge will be built, to the placing of tobacco into each of the holes where lodge poles will be inserted. When the lodge is completed, the rocks are placed in a pit ready for setting on fire. So was I taught in this traditional way.

We arrive at Family Camp with all the materials needed to construct the lodge. The materials used to make a contemporary lodge are different from those used in the past to construct many 'traditional' sweat lodges. I have chosen to use man-made materials such as hot water PVC pipe, painter's tarps, heavy black plastic – and even duct tape! My view is that it is not so much about what the lodge is made of – what is important is what happens during the ceremony. I use the PVC pipe to create the dome-shaped structure. Traditionally, the structure would be made from various types of long, slender saplings. Today, the covering of the lodge is made of tarps, blankets, and canvas. Traditional structures would have been covered with deer or bison hides, or even bark from trees.

I pray in the name of Jesus at every stage during construction. All people helping with the construction are blessed with the fanning of sage smoke over them. 'Smudging', seen as a symbolic form of purification, is the fanning of the sage smoke over the person. After the lodge is finished, we gather to pray and thank those who helped. In my tradition, both men and women have a part to play in the construction of the lodge.

It is my custom to teach the Sweat Lodge Ceremony 'from the ground up', including setup and breakdown. Many others who run sweat lodges only teach with an already-constructed lodge. Some 'legalistic' traditional Natives might call the materials I use 'wrong' because they are not natural or not done in their traditional way – because the construction materials are man-made. This is my response to this type of criticism: So you say my materials are 'not traditional'. Tell me, where are the bison and deer hides to cover your lodge? Did you use a hardware-store shovel to dig your fire pit? How about the galvanized water bucket and plastic ladle you use for dipping the water? How about the matches or lighter fluid you use to light your fire? Did you cut your saplings down with a stone ax or a hardware-store saw or ax? To them, some man-made materials are acceptable and some are not. Who is to say who is right? Traditionalism seems to be relative!

The Contextual Sweat Lodge Ceremony
Once the lodge is constructed, the leaders and attendees participate in the Sweat Lodge Ceremony. The ones who direct the ceremony are called 'conductors'. These leaders are made up of the contextual ministers who attend Family Camp. They come from many denominational backgrounds and have their own styles for conducting the ritual. Rocks are heated up in a fire just east of the entrance. There is teaching on what to expect during the ritual before entering the lodge. The male participants wear shorts and the women wear traditional sweat dresses, a skirt and t-shirt, or shorts and t-shirts, but a proper sense of modesty must be observed.

A water bucket with a ladle is brought in. It is used for pouring water onto the heated rocks which have been placed into a shallow pit in the center. The people enter by crawling into the lodge in a clockwise manner until everyone is inside. The conductor sits to the right of the doorway and the helper to the left. In my way of directing, the conductor or a designated singer leads the songs to the accompaniment of a Native hand drum. The helper or conductor transfers the heated rocks from the fire using a pitchfork. The rocks are then handed to him by the fire keeper – a person who is responsible to tend the fire and bring the heated rocks to the lodge with the pitch fork. The fire keeper is then asked in a traditional way by the conductor (with the presentation of tobacco) to care for the fire and the rocks. When everyone is in the lodge, a specific number of the rocks are brought in, as determined by the conductor. In this contextual Sweat Lodge Ceremony, I start with seven rocks and an additional six are brought in to make thirteen. Then three more may be brought in. The first seven rocks represent the seven directions (North, East, South, West, up, down, and center), honoring God's presence in all directions of creation. The thirteen represent Christ and the disciples. The final three represent the Father, Son, and Holy Spirit. The canvas door flap is brought down and the next stage of the ritual begins.

The 'Entering Phase' of a Rite of Passage ceremony is what has occurred so far. Once inside the lodge, the 'Liminal Phase' begins. While in the lodge, the participants sit in total darkness until I light a candle as the symbolic presence of the Holy Spirit; the light of the candle dispels the darkness. I use Scripture to introduce this imagery. Then I lead the group in an opening prayer and we participate in a contextual song using a Native hand drum (*an acceptable musical instrument*) and Christian lyrics. I say *musical instrument* because missionaries have imposed negative connotations on many Native cultural items, including drums, over the years.

With the first two stages of the service completed, I ask the participants to take turns introducing themselves and giving short prayer requests to be prayed over during the ceremony. I explain that they can pray in the name of Jesus here – because in many traditional sweat lodges the name of Jesus is not permitted. I further explain that this lodge has been blessed in the name of Jesus Christ, is set apart for Christian worship, and is a safe place for them be themselves and to pray. My opening prayer was an example to them as to how they can pray using the name of Christ. I then pour water on the heated rocks to create the steam which gives the participants a physical cleansing while they are also receiving a spiritual cleansing. When all have prayed, the first 'round' has been accomplished. We have breaks in the ceremony: Between each round, the door flap is opened to allow cool air in to refresh the people. During the next round, I spend some time and talk about whatever the Lord has placed on my heart. On the last round I lead a communion service using the water from the bucket and a tortilla or frybread (a traditional Native bread) as the elements. The communion service completes the ceremony and the participants exit the lodge.

This then ends the Liminal Phase, and the participants reintegrate into the world anew. They emerge from the dome of the lodge as a new creature – like a baby wet from the amniotic fluid of the womb. I say 'anew' because if they have never partaken in a contextual Sweat Lodge Ceremony before, their Christian world view has now expanded and a sense of freedom gained from the use of a contextual-style Native American ritual. They can now see and create a version of this ritual in their own ministry and tribal context with a greater sense of assurance that they are honoring Christ. They are further changed by seeing that the lies they were told about their cultural ways being evil and wrong have been dispelled. Because of my many years of experience in contextual ministry, they are comfortable taking these teachings and using them to reach the lost in their respective communities.

Contextual Prayer Rituals Using Incense: Holy Smoke

Incense burning is an integral part of the various rituals we conduct at Wiconi Family Camp. There are various occasions when 'smudging' is used during Family Camp: The blessing of the sweat lodges as they are constructed, the blessing of the auditorium where we hold our meetings, during our Sunrise Ceremony with the pipe each morning, the blessing of the drum before singers sing, the blessing of the Powwow grounds, and personal smudging ceremonies for individuals. This ritual can also take place in other situations as the need arises. These rituals are no different than those used when Old Testament Hebrew priests took incense from the Altar of Incense, which was next to the Holy of Holies, and blessed (or smudged) the Ark of the Covenant.

The steps used in the performance of these contextual rituals are similar in some respects and different in others. I will attempt to describe three of the most common rituals that have features in common with the others. I will talk about the personal Smudging Ceremony, the Sunrise Ceremony, and the blessing of the Pow-wow grounds.

The Contextual Personal Smudging Ceremony

In many cases this ceremony is done to begin a meeting or gathering. The spiritual leader's cedar box of medicines is brought out. The abalone shell, sage, and eagle fan are used. First I light the sage and bring it to a smolder, creating continual smoke. Then I smudge myself by pulling the smoke over myself with my hands and rendering a prayer. Then I begin fanning the smoke, starting at the east and moving clockwise. I walk in front of each person and if they are sitting, they will stand and accept the blessing by using their hands in a symbolic fashion, pulling the smoke over themselves – as if they were washing themselves with the smoke. If the person holds their hand up they want to be smudged, and if their hand stays on their lap, they are passed over in favor of the next person. If someone is unable to stand comfortably, I smudge them sitting down. In some cases people remove their glasses, which is fine because it was the way they were brought up. To remove the glasses is to bring yourself to a more natural state as a human being. One of the purposes of smudging for this type of gathering is to remove symbolically any negativity that might exist so as not to bring it into the meeting. This ensures that the meeting will run smoothly. This would include negative feelings such as resentment, guilt, disappointment, unresolved situations in their lives, and so on. Once each person is smudged, the meeting is ready to begin. I may place the shell and feather on the table, on the floor, or I may take the time to put everything away. This the basic method for conducting a Smudging Ceremony in a Native Christian contextual way. During the ceremony, those participating feel a sense of cleansing and a preparedness for the upcoming meeting. Not everyone experiences the same emotions. Some may feel renewed in their spirits, and each time they partake in the ceremony, they feel the sense of reverence that only comes with a smudging ritual.

The Contextual Sunrise Ceremony

I usually lead the Sunrise Ceremony at Family Camp. This ceremony takes place, as the name says, at sunrise. The ceremony can be conducted in several ways. The Navajo might use corn pollen and sprinkle it in a motion to the east, south, west, and the north, saying prayers for the new day. Natives of the Northern Woodlands might sprinkle tobacco in the same manner and say prayers as well. The Sunrise Ceremony with the pipe can be done in different ways depending upon the tribe. Because I am a Christian, I conduct the ceremony with references and prayers to Christ, whom I acknowledge as the Creator.

A Rite of Passage phase begins when I start the Sunrise Ceremony. There may be several people in attendance. We enter the ceremony when I open the cedar box containing the pipe bag and the medicines. Medicines here are not those you might purchase in a pharmacy, but are natural plants Native people use for their aroma when burned as incense. These medicines are sage, sweet grass, cedar, and tobacco. Incense smoke is made by setting the medicine on fire, blowing out the flame, and then allowing the medicine to smolder in an abalone shell. This creates the smoke used for the blessing and for sending up prayers to the Creator. I use tobacco, but some will use a mixture of grasses, barks, and tobacco. I was taught to use the pipe by three traditional elders and they all used tobacco.

The Liminal Phase begins when I lay out the pipe bowl, pipe stem, shell, and eagle feather. I then light the sage in the shell and bless each item to be used in the ceremony, and also myself. After smudging, I pray over the tobacco and then give it to an assistant to distribute to the attendees. When each person has taken some of the tobacco, they put it back into a pouch which I will use for the ceremony. At this point I put the pipe bowl and the stem together, which symbolically creates the center of the universe. In this way, God's attention is directed to this group gathered for Early Morning Prayer. With the sage still smoldering, I take a pinch of the tobacco and bless it and point the pinch of tobacco in my fingers to the east, then place it into the pipe bowl. I repeat this action through the other directions, including toward the ground and to the sky. In doing this I am *not* praying to these directions, to the spirits, or to the symbols some tribes place on each direction. I pray to the Creator in each direction because the Creator is in every direction. I point to myself as a seventh direction, because Creator-Jesus is also in me. Once the pipe is lit, I bless myself with the smoke from the pipe and then repeat by pointing the pipe and a puff of smoke into the air toward each direction. I finish by pointing it to myself. I do not share my pipe to be smoked by others; I am the only one who smokes it. I close the ceremony by praying with words for the people attending and then dismiss the group.

At this point, the Liminal Phase ends and the attendees reenter the world, having participated in the Pipe Ceremony with appreciation for the prayers symbolically sent up in the smoke to God.

The Contextual Blessing of the Powwow Grounds

The purpose of this ceremony is to prepare the Powwow grounds for the day's events. Prayers are said for good weather, safe travel for those coming to the Powwow, that God's name will be honored at this event, that friendships will be made or rekindled, and that this piece of earth will be set apart today to bring glory to Jesus.

This ceremony begins by opening my cedar box and taking out the abalone shell, the sage, and the eagle fan. Standing in the middle of the Powwow circle, I light the sage to a smolder and with the eagle fan I bless myself by fanning the smoke over my head three times. After blessing myself as I did in the Pipe Ceremony, I fan the smoke from the sage to the seven directions. At this point I walk to the eastern side of the circle where the participants will enter the Powwow grounds and fan the smoke to the directions and to the sky. I repeat this action to the south, west, and north. I return to the center of the Powwow grounds and close with a silent prayer to Jesus. If there are workers in the area, they will come up to me for a blessing with the smoke. When all have been blessed I put out the smoke and return the items back to the cedar box. This ends the blessing and at this time the workers can begin to set up for the Powwow.

Contextualization of Native Social and Spiritual Practices

Native Christians and Powwow Dancing

In the past, Native Americans who wanted to participate in Powwow dancing faced strong disapproval from the Church – not because the dances actually were wrong or evil, but because they were perceived as such by missionaries and church people from other cultural backgrounds. Why? Because these practices were different from the missionary's ways and therefore seen as suspicious and pagan, not to be used in any way as an expression of Christian faith. The Powwow is mainly a social dance event and takes place in a community. The social dances of the white missionaries take place in their communities – there is no difference. Powwow dancing is social dancing. It is a way for the Native person to tell a story. For example, my style of dancing is the Men's Northern Traditional. In the dance I tell a story of a battle in war times or hunting an animal for food. I act out the stories with various steps and arm movements to illustrate the tale of a hunt or battle. During the dance I tell about the way I fought, or the way I went about tracking down and finally killing the animal.

The process of becoming a dancer in the Powwow world is a Rite of Passage. Some take the time to learn it and enter the dance circle in the right way. Some do not even know there is a protocol for becoming a dancer and step into the circle without taking the time to do it properly. Becoming a dancer begins with a desire to do so, and then the person seeks out a mentor to help them learn what it means to become a dancer. The Liminal Phase is entered when the person starts the journey to becoming a dancer. This is the time spent with the mentor making the dance regalia, learning the meanings behind the dance style, and learning the different songs you may be dancing to. You also learn the history behind your style of dance. For example: with the Jingle Dress style, you learn where the style came from, why there are metal cones (jingles) used in the making of the dress, and the reason it is a prayer style of dance – and a much respected style of dancing too. When the preparation is completed, the person is taken by the mentor to the dance circle. The mentor requests permission to take some time during the event in order to welcome the new dancer into the circle – the conducting of the 'coming-out' dance ceremony. A respected person is asked to speak on behalf of the new dancer because speaking for themselves is seen as boastful, and humility is stressed. The person who speaks on behalf of the dancer can talk about their good traits and their accomplishments.

The final step to becoming a dancer in the Powwow circle is to dance. This first dance is very ceremonial, and the other dancers trained in your style join you after you make one trip around the circle. Then, all the other dancers of your style join you for one 'dance-time' together. (This practice can differ from tribe to tribe). Sometimes those with the same style will dance with the initiate at their first dance. After the first dance, the community comes into the Powwow circle, welcomes you as a dancer, and then joins you in one more dance around the circle. The Liminal Phase is now complete – you are now a dancer. Thus begins the Reintegration Phase of the Rite of Passage, which is done with a traditional 'giveaway'. The Reintegration Phase is a process of extending honor to others by giving rather than receiving gifts. The giveaway is our Native way of showing our appreciation to those in attendance. During the giveaway, distribution of gifts begins with the most honored people. These are usually the head staff, the emcee, the arena director, the head dancers, and the elders. Then you give gifts to the rest of the community. A closing word is then said by the appointed spokesperson, along with a thank you to the Powwow committee for allowing you to have this opportunity.

Contextual Singing with the Drum

Native drums have been falsely accused of association with evil spirits for far too long. Here is a story about how I believe the Native drum got this misleading and negative reputation. The story says that when the drum was being played in deepest, darkest, jungles, somewhere, there was evil spirit activity going on. From that point on, the drum was accused of 'drawing up evil spirits'. It was not the drum that drew the spirits into the place, it was the act of asking (summoning) them to come that made them come – not the drum. The drum just happened to be playing when the spirits were invoked. If any other musical instrument would had been playing at the time, then that would be the instrument associated with evil spirit activity. My thought is this, 'If a piano was being played in the jungle at the time, would that instrument also be associated with drawing up evil spirit activity?' How ridiculous!

Singing along with the hand drum or the big drum can be a part of many Native rituals and ceremonies. The hand drum is mainly an individual instrument, and the big drum is for groups to sit around to play and sing. Sometimes individuals play their own hand drums at the same time others play the big drum. I have used the hand drum in church services, in the sweat lodge, at funerals, weddings, and Powwows. The big drum is played by a group, mostly at Powwows, to provide the music for the various dance styles. The big drum may be the only instrument used in a contextual church service. The Brethren in Christ Mission uses the big drum as the main instrument in their Sunday worship service. There are now many types of songs composed by contextual musicians that are available to be sung with the big drum: honor songs, worship songs, flag songs, and prayer songs.

The Process of Contextualizing Sacred Rituals and Ceremonies

The incorporation of the contextual expressions of faith described above might be seen as innovations within the Christian world – but were not necessarily considered for use as adaptations to implement change. Each is intended to reinforce to Christian Native Americans that they can be redeemed from the lies told them about their culture and thus be brought into Christ-honoring expressions of their heritage. We incorporated these adapted rituals (from their long neglected and lost traditions) for use at Wiconi Family Camp to meet the need for meaningful expressions of Christian faith among Native American people. We hope to replace Western Christian traditions which have lost their meaning – if they ever had any – for First Nations people. We were taught that the Western tradition of Christian faith was '*the* way of doing things'. This worked for some people. But others are now beginning to realize they never had to *lose* their Native identity to *become* Christians. They are seeing their traditions used within a safe environment where experimentation is accepted and encouraged. We desire to see the contextualization of our traditions (their change and adaptation) meet the needs of the future to reach people more effectively for Christ.

Now, can the use of contextualized Native rituals meet the needs of Native people in this new paradigm – a paradigm where their rituals and ceremonies are now close to being accepted expressions of their faith in Jesus? When we look at the historical path of evangelism among Native people we see a dismal story. The government and the Church worked toward eradicating many of the sacred rituals and ceremonies used by Native people. They were told to accept the religion and spiritual ways of their oppressors. Thus the sacred 'prayer ways' used by Native people were replaced with another culture's way of praying. When we begin to work from a contextual paradigm, many avenues to presenting the gospel of Christ are made available.

The ritual of the sweat lodge was used for generations by Native people, and it gave them a way to relate to the spiritual world and to strengthen relationships within their communities. The contextual approach to presenting the gospel to Native people permits a return to the familiar rituals of their ancestors. Within this approach we can now use the same ritual; but, instead of the Native person praying to the spirit world and the gods they were familiar with before their faith in Christ, they can now use the ritual to pray to the true God known in the person of Jesus Christ. The original functions (purification, prayer, strengthening of relationships) remain, but in a Christ-honoring way.

This is my starting point for ministry to Native people at the Brethren in Christ Mission and also at Wiconi Family Camp. In each I have taken the liberty of creating new versions of older rituals. I have begun to see changes taking place in the lives of Native people.

I have mentioned that the Sweat Lodge Ceremony at Overcomers and at Wiconi Family Camp is an example of the Rite of Passage. The clients or camp attendees enter this ritual in the Liminal Phase where life changes can take place. In the Liminal Phase, trust is built between the staff and clients, a new view of the ceremony is gained, and a feeling of normalcy is sensed as the ritual used by their ancestors is now used for their worship to Christ. I notice in the sweat lodge that when the clients pray, a sense of catharsis happens, and the prayers said in the lodge indicate a renewed and welcomed connection with the Creator. The addition of heat and steam is a pleasing experience with a sense of cultural normalcy. This way of prayer – long denied to Native peoples – has now been revived for their use as an expression of their Christian faith.

Similar spiritual experiences which have occurred during Sweat Lodge Ceremonies are described by clients of the Overcomers program and attendees at Family Camp. Both ministries include contextually-adapted ceremonies which encourage growth and exemplify a renewal of Native ritual in a Christian way. Similarly, the use of incense in prayer rituals is making a comeback – it is a ritual included in both the Sweat Lodge Ceremony and the Pipe Ceremony. Several people said that they feel their prayers are 'stronger' when included with the Pipe Ceremony. When I conduct the Pipe Ceremony, I pass a wooden bowl of tobacco so that all those wishing to participate may take a pinch in their hand and pray with it, and then add the tobacco to another wooden bowl. I then take some of the combined mixture of the returned tobacco and place it in the pipe which I will smoke to the directions sending up their prayers. The act of prayer with group participation brings about a sense of community, knowing that prayers from the entire group are being sent to God. When I conduct the Pipe Ceremony, I act as a priest doing a pastoral prayer during a church service. Each time people participate in this style of prayer, they become more comfortable with the use of incense.

As Christians, we acknowledge that God knows our prayers even before we ask because He knows our hearts. The use of the rituals and ceremonies among Native people gives them a comfortable place from which to worship in prayer – giving them the needed symbolism to connect culturally with their heritage. This is not unique to Native people. Similar rituals and symbolic actions are used within our modern-day churches. Examples of these are: filling out prayer cards for the pastor to read aloud, raising hands to symbolize an unspoken prayer, verbally sharing a prayer request with the group, sharing prayers with a prayer chain, the playing of soft music during prayer time, raising hands while praying, kneeling with hands folded and head bowed, and the lighting of candles. There are probably many more.

Learning to be a Powwow dancer is also a spiritual journey and brings fulfillment to many. Over the past few years that we have been participating in and then directing Family Camp, we have had the honor of bringing dancers into the Powwow circle for their first dance ceremonies. This is a big step in their spiritual journeys, and when Christ is at the center, it can be the needed boost for their spiritual development. Playing and singing with the Native drum can have the same spiritual effect on those who want to use the drum as an expression of their Christian faith. We all know singing the old Christian hymns we grew up with is meaningful to us. Over the years, the newer contextual songs have become as meaningful as the old hymns I grew up hearing. This has also become true among those attending our Family Camp events. I have stood near the stage by the performers and watched the audience following the contextual lyrics as they sang along.

To encourage the use of these rituals as accepted practices was a challenge and it took much discernment and prayer – not to mention a deep understanding of these rituals themselves. We realize there is nothing salvific in these or any cultural rituals, but they are useful in that their symbolic meanings are understood by the Indigenous users. These types of change and transition require a liminal period to process the implemented ritual. This Liminal Phase is a natural place for experimentation and trial and error to take place – and an acceptable ritual for use within the emerging contextual Native American community.

Survey of the Spiritual Impact of the Wiconi Family Camp/Powwow

I interviewed ten Wiconi Family Camp attendees in order to learn about their perceptions of the success and impact of Family Camp over the past ten years. Several themes became evident both in the Wiconi and BICO Alcohol Treatment Program research.

The importance of the formation of family and Christian relationships was number one. Several of the Family Camp participants said the camp made them feel like they were part of a family. The camp is advertised as a 'Family Camp', and those attending are made up of many Native families and others who are directly involved in some form of Native Christian ministry. In the beginning, Family Camp was a place for these ministers to meet and develop relationships with those who were also struggling 'in the trenches' of contextual ministry. Due to this commonality, many are blessed and grow deeply in their relationship with Christ and each other. Both campers and staff grow in their faith. Being around other believers was seen as very important in their faith journeys.

When we decided to open the Powwow to the public, the local people attending also noticed the family-friendly, relational feeling already sensed by camp attendees. One community member from Turner, Oregon said, 'We like the way you Christians put on a Powwow'. The Powwow has many audience participation dances. The 'Intertribal dance' is for everyone and people can dance with or without regalia. Another dance offered is the 'Switch Dance' where a lady dancer will place her shawl on the back of a male friend or guest, and that person has to dance ladies-style. This creates a very fun and enjoyable time with much laughter. One other dance is the 'Potato Dance' where a couple places a potato between their foreheads and tries to dance without the potato falling. The winner is the last couple dancing with the potato still between their foreheads. All of the above-mentioned events highlight the importance of social relationships at the camp and Powwow.

Spiritual growth is encouraged during the presentation times at Family Camp when invited speakers share their experiences in ministry. Questions relating to the importance of a biblical foundation of contextual ministry are dealt with and answered. The presentations are filled with biblical examples and give the attendees a real boost in their faith journeys. More than one has said, 'I have never seen that in Scripture before'. In 2014, the camp's theme focused on the music ministries of several of our contextual leaders. I asked the speakers to discuss the good, bad, and ugly aspects of their ministry journeys and conclude with the upside of their ministry experiences – by sharing the many positive features of contextual music ministry. These presentations offer a look into the real-life situations of the musicians and, in so doing, help build the attendees' individual faith journeys. Many see the importance of a contextual program-style to meet the needs of the attendees. When asked about how they perceived the program, one responded, 'The style of the camp is just what is needed for learning how to be contextual'.

The Sweat Lodge Ceremony is another cultural tradition used at Family Camp to increase spiritual development. Both the history and construction of the lodge are taught. If they wish, camp attendees may participate (and are encouraged to do so) in one of the Sweat Lodge Ceremonies conducted by qualified ministers. I offer a Sweat Lodge Ceremony for beginners. In this ritual for beginners, I keep the heat in the lodge lower than those offered for the more experienced in a ritual Sweat Lodge Ceremony. In addition to the beginner's sweat, Lora and I offer a co-ed 'healing' sweat which we conduct for both young and old. It has been my practice to set the age limit for participation to twelve and older. Keeping the lodge temperature lower for those attending makes the lodge environment a safe place to learn the basics of the ritual. In this ceremony my wife Lora and I encourage the participants to open up about some of their mental, physical, emotional, and spiritual issues so we may pray for them right there. In so doing, the sweat lodge becomes a very important place for spiritual healing of many of those attending. After participating in these ceremonies, all those responding said they recognized a sense of restoration that helped them in their spiritual development.

Many Family Camp attendees see the use of Native musical instruments as an important factor in spiritual growth. The staff and presenters affirm the usefulness of the drum songs sung by Native Christian men. Several shared how they are learning the contextual songs, and how these songs have become an important part of their lives. They also said other instruments including rattles, flutes, and drums are useful in the song services. The drum has been a fixture at Wiconi Family Camp from the beginning. Many Christians fear the use of the Native drum in Christian worship. At Family Camp, the drum is prayed over and the songs sung on it have Christian lyrics. Many of the fears about the drum dissipate during worship times, as we intentionally promote a positive image of the drums and singing in a Native style. Fear is replaced with good feelings about the drum and many are then comfortable with its use and even participate in the songs.

My findings revealed a view of the rituals and ceremonies as truly sacred to the attendees of Family Camp and Powwow. I was delighted to hear a young couple say 'they will keep coming back to learn more' from my teachings.

The Rites of Passage Theme at Wiconi Family Camp

My world of contextual ministry is so familiar to me, it makes it hard to sometimes convey to others what we are actually trying to accomplish within the Native American Contextualization Movement. In my study, I had to look for deeper themes running through the responses. I also looked for themes from Rites of Passage in data from both the Wiconi Family Camp and the Brethren in Christ Overcomers program, and there were many commonalities. The Rites of Passage theme showed up in both.

Over half of those questioned mentioned concepts connected with the theme of entering and exiting the Liminal Phase. It is important to notice that the Overcomer's clients enter a three-month residential program and the Family Camp attendees enter a much shorter, but structurally similar three-day time of liminal passage. More than one Family Camp participant said that when arriving at the camp they had a feeling that, 'Something about this camp is going to be different'. In ceremonies where Rites of Passage are taking place, time-frames vary. They can happen in hours or days, and others such as the treatment program can take months. While the Overcomers clients are isolated from the outside world, the attendees at Family Camp separate themselves voluntarily when they register for the camp. Seventy-five percent said that the period of isolation is what makes these events more productive in people's lives. One camper said, 'These three days feel like a whole week'. Separation and isolation are the first stages of Rites of Passage, the 'Entering Phase'. As the attendees become more comfortable with the environment, they gain a sense of freedom as they learn new concepts. Sixty-two percent of those questioned affirmed this. Many also said they felt that the camp was a safe place for them to learn. This new information comes from presentations and the actual practice of rituals they had only ever heard of and were not allowed to practice in their churches. As the attendees became comfortable, they began to become more aware of a new identity within their reach and began to make it their own. With every new experience they encounter in ritual and ceremony, this new Christian identity blossoms. Change and transition begin to occur with 62% saying ritual and ceremony are very important. One camper said, 'I now feel proud to be a Native'. By the end of the camp, the attendees stated how the camp had changed their view of themselves and in the way they live out a truly Native Christian lifestyle. Some of these positive experiences take place when campers attend their first Christian-led sweat lodge. Other turning points occur for campers when they see second or third-year attendees dancing at the Powwow in full regalia. It impacts them when they realize that these Native people are believers in Jesus Christ.

There are many parallels noticed when comparing the data gathered at the BICO Alcohol Treatment Program and Wiconi Family Camp and Powwow. I believe that the bottom line is that if we can let ourselves begin to see that all life is sacred and allow Native people – whether at the camp or the treatment program – to live freely in their Native skin, many Rites of Passage will be experienced.

The results of the research are compelling and indicate that contextual approaches should continue to be integrated into Native ministry. Dr Richard Twiss was one of the forerunners of this movement. After his passing, the Wiconi staff and board faced a period of change and transition. They persevered, not knowing what Wiconi would eventually become. Twiss and his colleagues were able to create, with the guidance of the Holy Spirit, a contextual approach to ministry they felt was needed to create a preferred future for our Native communities.

There are few creative thinkers of this caliber, but they are among us. As the current Director of Wiconi, I'm honored to use the skills I have been granted to help move Wiconi into the future. This journey will continue to be a process. 'Creative thinkers are relatively few (two to five percent of the population), but we don't need many of them to make an exciting and stimulating world. They are the out-of-the-box thinkers, artists, inventers and prophets.[4] I never thought I would be included in such a group.

---

[4] Alan Nelson and Gene Appel, *How to Change Your Church (Without Killing It)* (Nashville, TN: Thomas Nelson Publishing Group, 2000), p. 75.

6

ANALYSIS AND COMPARISON OF THE BICO AND WICONI MINISTRIES: THEMES AND RITUAL PROCESS

The purpose for conducting the research at the Brethren in Christ Overcomers (BICO) Alcohol Treatment Program was to discover the factors that contributed to the men's recovery and whether contextual methods had a significant part in this process. I had initially spent a large amount of time seeking out the efficacy of contextual methods and missed some other realities that were present. In the re-analysis, I began to notice several commonalities clearly emerging from the data: (1) The importance the participants placed on the program's use of Bible instruction, (2) The influence of the Christian lifestyle of the staff members who interacted with the clients, and (3) The influence of 'Rites of Passage' in view of the effect of a liminal passage.

In my analysis of the Wiconi Family Camp ministry, I discovered that the same three themes were evident. As noted when studying the BICO data, the importance the participants placed on both programs' use of Bible instruction had greater significance than the contextual use of ritual, although it was shown to be important as well. At Family Camp the influence of the Christian lifestyle of the staff was also influential. The theme of Rites of Passage was also there. These two programs – although very different – both illustrate a journey through Rites of Passage. Both ministries encourage individuals to seek a more positive way of life and how to be better people as Native Christians. They also provide an exploration of the rituals and ceremonies that can lead to becoming a new creation in Christ.

During my work with the BICO program, I discovered that biblical instruction is greatly reinforced as it is modelled by the Christian lifestyles of the staff as they interact with them daily. A Rite of Passage is a journey that is described by Victor Turner as including the Separation Phase, the Liminal Phase, and the Reaggregation Phase.[1] The Separation Phase begins when the clients enter the program. The three months spent in the program comprise the Liminal Phase. The reintegration (Reaggregation Phase) of the clients occurs as they enter the world once again. They become pilgrims entering a journey, having been physically, mentally, emotionally, and spiritually changed through a Rite of Passage.

Attendees at Wiconi Family Camp also journey through a Rite of Passage ceremony. They separate from home to enter the program during registration time. Three days at Family Camp represents the Liminal Phase, and the ending of Family Camp indicates their Reaggregation into the world. Wiconi Family Camp was established on biblical principles guided by the Holy Spirit. Richard Twiss was able to create – with the help of colleagues – a unique space where lives could be changed in community with other Native people. Family Camp is a place where individuals can enter the program (Separation Phase), experience immersion in contextual life ways in the company of others who fully embrace that lifestyle (the Liminal Phase), and end with a closing ceremony and then re-integrate (Reaggregation) into the world as contextual, maturing Christians. This whole experience shows the marks of a Rites of Passage journey with rituals and ceremonies designed to renew an individual's mind as they consider the contextual paradigm.

The data collected from individual and group interviews revealed similarities and differences in both the BICO Alcohol Treatment Program and Wiconi Family Camp. The rituals and ceremonies to be discussed will include the 'contextual' use of the Sweat Lodge Ceremony, the Pipe Ceremony, Powwow Dancing, singing with the drum, and the Smudging Ritual. I emphasize *con-*

---

[1] Roxburgh, *The Missionary Congregation*, p. 27.

textual because these same ceremonies and rituals are conducted in Native communities by individuals who do not profess faith in Jesus.[2] These five ceremonies/rituals are used in both programs. I will examine them and compare their use in the BICO program and Family Camp, looking at them from the viewpoint of Rites of Passage as being critical to spiritual development. The areas of comparison will focus on biblical instruction, the importance of the Christian lifestyle of the staff, and the influence of the concept of Rites of Passage. At the same time I will look at their effect on the sense of the sacred and ceremony that take place in the Liminal Phase of a Rite of Passage. One more area I became aware of from the BICO and Family Camp programs was that the use of cultural elements gave a positive view of Native heritage and increased the self-esteem of the clients and campers.

The Rite of Passage theme was not included in my first analysis as I was seeking only the effectiveness of contextual approaches. But when I allowed myself to take a much closer look at the data, I found evidence of the use of Rites of Passage, a theme that seems to be a major part of a client's recovery or a camper's spiritual development. A successful journey through a Rite of Passage is the key to recovery and spiritual development in Christ – not just the integration of ritual and ceremony.

The Sweat Lodge Ceremony

The incorporation of several rituals and practices in the Sweat Lodge Ceremony – also called 'the sweat' – creates an environment of relationship and the building of trust. The Sweat Lodge Ceremony at the BICO program has become a prominent part of its approach to recovery. Similarly, at Family Camp, the Sweat Lodge Ceremony builds relationship and trust. The sweat lodges at the Brethren in Christ program and the Wiconi Family Camp are constructed by the participants, and traditional stories are shared about the origins of the sweat and its use both traditionally

---

[2] I am saying that the rituals and ceremonies I am using have been thought through prayerfully, scripturally, and theologically, utilizing critical contextualization with praxis to create new forms. As a practitioner, these meanings reflect my Christian beliefs and not those of a non-Christian practitioner.

and contextually. The Christian symbolism used in both venues helps dispel the fears surrounding non-Christian use of ceremony.

I conduct the Sweat Lodge Ceremony using many of the elements of the *non-contextual* Sweat Lodge Ceremony. The adaptations I have implemented were included as a result of several years of searching scripture for guidance and experimenting with contextual methods. The ritual uses the dome-shaped structure built in much the same fashion as most traditional lodges. I use lava rocks heated in an open fire. As noted earlier, I do not get caught up in the legalistic way a lodge should be made, and I choose to use hot water PVC plumbing pipe in the dome's construction. The reason I do this is because it is not so much what the lodge is made of, it's about the prayers that are said inside that I focus on during this 'nowhere time'. I do not overemphasize the darkness, which is characteristic in a traditional lodge – instead I incorporate a small candle during the ceremony. Doing this dispels the darkness as I share how the flame is a symbol of the Holy Spirit. The participants – most of whom are new to the experience – feel more at ease with the use of the candle which helps create a safe environment. I have been in traditional lodges and the sense of the darkness is an uneasy feeling – like being underground. Further, I do not call on the 'spirits' (plural), but only upon God the Holy Spirit to be in our presence as we journey together. This too brings a sense of safety that enables Christian newcomers to the sweat to participate more fully.

I do conduct the sweat at a high temperature for those who are familiar with my method because they are more knowledgeable about the contextual ritual and used to the heat. For first-timers I use a lower temperature so as not to have anyone leave the lodge due to too much discomfort. This allows newcomers to see the potential of the sweat lodge for being a very positive place for sharing prayers. My main focus is on *prayer* and not on the sweat lodge as an endurance test. There is a place for the 'hot' Sweat Lodge Ceremony, but for my purposes I focus on the act of prayer and the healing process that can take place for those who have felt threatened by traditional sweats. Sometimes the more conditioned participants, those who are used to a hot lodge, unintentionally create a sense of competition. I conduct the 'lower heat' sweat at both the Overcomers program and Family Camp. In these two contextual sweat lodges, Rites of Passage are experienced. The Sweat Lodge Ceremony is a sacred ritual/ceremony that can be seen as a separate Rite of Passage ceremony in and of itself. There is the preparation time before entering; the actual entering (Entering Phase); the time spent in the lodge (Liminal Phase); the ending of the ceremony; the emerging from the sweat lodge; and the re-integrating back into the world. The Overcomers program can be seen as a Rite of Passage ceremony as can the overall Wiconi Family Camp program. The Sweat Lodge Ceremony within each can essentially be a 'Rite of Passage' ceremony within the greater ones of the programs themselves.

Probably the most significant aspect of the Sweat Lodge Ceremony that I conduct happens during the conclusion when we celebrate the Lord's Supper using the pattern from Lk. 22.1-23. I have the freedom to design a communion service using unleavened Indian frybread or tortillas as the host. Instead of wine, we drink the water from the bucket used for pouring on the heated rocks. I started doing the Lord's Supper this way because of my dream/vision where I saw the Eucharist being performed (untouched by Western influences) by a young Native boy on his vision quest. During this boy's vision quest, it was revealed to him why Christ had to die. In honor of this vision, he took the cooked meat of a rabbit and a shell filled with water and acted out the Lord's Supper without strictly following the actual biblical account of the Last Supper. He had celebrated an *Indigenous* Eucharistic service! Because of this I teach the clients about the freedom we have to participate in a contextual communion service, and how frybread or tortillas can represent and be symbolic of the actual body of Christ, and the water from the bucket can represent His blood.

I have had many years of experience conducting the contextual Sweat Lodge Ceremony at the Overcomers program. Overcomers was my proving ground for the development of this ceremony with the focus on prayer to Christ, the use of a candle, innovative construction materials, and the use of the Lord's Supper as part of the closing. The time I spent with the Overcomers before working with Wiconi Family Camp made all the difference in its acceptance. When Richard Twiss heard about my method, he invited us into the Wiconi ministry. What Richard was able to do in promoting the concepts and the philosophical awareness of contextual methods, I was able to do in actual practice as a Native insider, being both a Christian and a traditional practitioner.

Knowledge gained throughout the entire sweat can be immense, unspoken, and even a subliminal experience. The clients at Overcomers and the people at Family Camp learn so much both actively and vicariously – we try to teach the protocols that Native people like myself know and take for granted. When a newcomer experiences the event, they engage in active learning that can only come from participation. It is in the many nuances encountered during the ceremony that make the Sweat Lodge Ceremony a Rite of Passage. Many have mentioned that they felt the presence of God while participating in the contextual version of the ritual. Many also said that the contextual ceremony was not as 'scary' as they had expected it to be, and that it was a way to honor God in prayer in a fully Indigenous manner. They believed that the presence of the sweat lodge in the context of a Christian camp was a natural fit for the camp's overall structure. Many acknowledged that the ceremony – with its incorporation of their culture into Christian worship – became an authentic expression of their personal faith.

The Pipe Ceremony

As with the Sweat Lodge Ceremony, there are traditional ways to use the pipe among many tribes, and each is sacred and used with the utmost humility and respect. The use of the pipe in the contextual manner has many of the same features found in its traditional use. One important requirement is keeping an orthodox usage protocol. That is, if a pipe is handed down to someone in the same tribe, the traditional Pipe Ceremony taught by the Pipe Carrier to an apprentice must be performed in the exact tradition and protocol of the teacher. Each tribe can have its own particular method of performing the Pipe Ceremony. The way they care for the pipe also holds true for the new contextual Pipe Ceremony.

All Indigenous sacred traditions have developed and changed over the centuries. Culture is not static – it is dynamic and has changed throughout history. That is, at one point within a culture there was an *established* tradition, and then at another point a *new* tradition was introduced. According to our oral stories, there was a specific time when the Pipe and Sweat Lodge Ceremonies were given or taught to the people – showing that those ceremonies did not exist before then – they were new traditions. So, it should be no surprise that 'new' contextual traditions have come into use.

I have developed a contextual Pipe Ceremony that reflects both my Native American heritage and my Christian faith. I entered into this journey by seeking guidance from the Lord and the guidance of three Anishinaabe elders in their traditional use of the pipe. ('Anishinaabe' is the word for the people who made up the three tribes of the Great Lakes region known as the Ottawa, Potawatomi, and the Ojibway). After sharing my calling and desire to learn the use of the pipe, each elder granted me their *personal* permission – not the permission of their tribe – to use the pipe as a follower of the Jesus way. The description of the use of the pipe in a contextual manner does not follow any strict protocol of the Anishinaabe tribes, but instead *incorporates* the traditional usage, which is keeping the protocol of the ceremony intact while creating new meanings for those functions. With this foundation established, I began to use the Pipe Ceremony as part of my sacred journey as I walk my Native traditional and Christian paths together.

When I recognized that I could personally use the Pipe Ceremony in a Christ-honoring way, I also realized it could be used in the BICO program and at Family Camp. With the Overcomers program I incorporate the Pipe Ceremony in conjunction with several aspects of the recovery program's Sweat Lodge Ceremony. From time to time when asked to speak at the Mission Sunday worship service, I conduct and teach the use of the Pipe in a contextual manner. Each month I am invited to conduct the Sweat Lodge Ceremony for the clients as part of their treatment program and also join them as they gather around the drum that is positioned next to the sweat lodge. During this time we sing several contextual songs. As we sing the last song – which is a special song in the Native traditional setting called the 'pipe loading' song – I prepare the pipe for the ceremony. At the beginning of the song I open my cedar box which contains an abalone shell in which to burn the sage used to bless the pipe, the tobacco, and all associated items for the ceremony. I start by offering the men the tobacco I will use. The men take some of the tobacco and then return it back into a separate bowl from which I will load the pipe. This is a symbolic way for them to place their prayers *into* the tobacco I will use in the ceremony. I use the same ritual for Wiconi Family Camp participants.

At the Overcomers program most of the men do not have a saving relationship with Jesus. They may have been brought up with some Christian understanding, but for the most part these men need Jesus in their lives. However, with Family Camp, many, but not all of those attending, are professing believers in Jesus. In both ministries I conduct the ceremony the same way, always expressing the need for all to look toward Jesus so they will receive Him as their Savior.

At Family Camp I also conduct what is called the 'Sunrise Ceremony', an early morning Pipe Ceremony where campers are invited to attend so they can start their day centered on Christ.

To understand the Pipe Ceremony in contextual ministry and its relationship to spiritual development as a sacred time of liminality, we need to look at it as a Rite of Passage. During the Rite of Passage, sacred space is created with the beginning of the Pipe Ceremony – this is the Entering Phase. The Liminal Phase begins when new information is gained, and those attending open themselves to change and transition in their lives. Biblical instruction is given, offering the participants the opportunity to grow in their spiritual lives. In many cases – both at Overcomers and Family Camp – positive self-image and self-esteem start to grow in their lives. When giving biblical instruction, I use a combination of my Christian faith and the spiritual rituals of my Native beliefs. For example, when I conduct the Pipe Ceremony I place tobacco in the bowl for burning and have the smoke rise toward heaven. In Native traditions when a pinch is taken and placed in the bowl, it is blessed and pointed to six directions: east, south, west, north, to the sky, and to the ground. In this traditional way, the direction is associated with either father sky, mother earth, mountain, thunder, the sun, or even spirits. In my contextual method, I point to each of these directions, but I only associate them with God's omnipresence in each direction.

At Family Camp I offer a special teaching time on the contextual usage of incense and the Pipe Ceremony. In this class I open the Bible and share my journey toward my understanding of contextual ministry. What makes my class and ministry with Wiconi unique? As far as I know, I am the only contextual leader to openly use the Pipe Ceremony as a significant aspect of ministry. As a person who uses the pipe, I know not all are considered 'Pipe Carriers'. This is an official position given to someone who is regarded as a person of respect and integrity and seeks to follow a godly life. Pipe Carriers do not call themselves that – they are designated as such by their community.

In Table 1, I show how the use of ritual affects a person's life. The Pipe Ceremony is a powerful and sacred ritual. Most men at Overcomers understand the sacred nature of the ceremony, and when it is conducted they show it due respect. At Family Camp most new attendees do not understand the sacredness of the pipe, and this is why I offer the class. After eleven years of using the pipe at Family Camp, I have earned respect as someone who uses it in a contextual manner, but also as one who is a believer in Jesus Christ. The innovation that takes place through this understanding is the awareness that tradition and ceremony can actually be taken from within the Native traditional world, redeemed for the honor of our Lord Jesus Christ, and used in Christian ministry in all good conscience.

Powwow Dancing

This area of contextual ministry is exciting mostly because it is full of flash and glitter along with style and performance. Native dancing was once viewed as a 'no-no' by many Christian denominations. I could never see the problem with dance because I look at it from a different cultural perspective. Dance is a common part of almost every culture. Just taking a minute to search the Internet for 'dance in Europe' will show many different styles. Not to have this tradition in the Church is sad. We in the contextual ministry movement see the benefits of the use of dance. Many of the styles used among Indigenous peoples tell their stories. Micronesian people from the South Pacific have attended Family Camp for several years, and we have seen firsthand the beauty of their dances, performed by both men and women. Dance styles in the Native American world vary across the North American continent. Dance is a part of our family life, and not having it as part of our Christian life would be hard to imagine.

Powwow dancing is a type of Native American dancing that can be competitive or social. The outfits the dancers make and wear are called 'regalia'. Some who are unfamiliar with Powwow dancing often call these outfits 'costumes'. Costumes are worn to pretend to be something else, such as during Halloween time when children dress as goblins or as superheroes. In the Native American world, regalia represent the people and their way of life. They are not called costumes because they signify *who* the dancer is. We are not pretending to be something else – we are being *who* we are. For us, dancing is not unique or unusual – it is a way of life.

As far as seeing dancing as being biblical I say, 'What's the problem?' Sure, there are dances that are associated with drunken celebrations or 'the dark side', regardless of the culture they come from. I am not considering these types of dances. The ones I am discussing are those mentioned throughout many sections of scripture as being used for rejoicing and praise. Still today the Hebrew people have traditional dances that are practiced when celebrating various Rites of Passage. The Hebrew people of the Bible reference dancing at various times in scripture – the most notable being done by Miriam after crossing the Red Sea on dry land as the Hebrews escaped from Egypt (Exod. 15.20-21). Native American people have had dancing throughout their history too. Every culture has some style of dance – some for celebration and some for evil. Some dances are for celebration and some are for evil. Within the Native American world, the majority of dances are for the good, but I admit there are those used for evil as well.

Although it is not part of the formal program, at Overcomers I do teach about Powwow dancing and present my form of the

Men's Northern Traditional dancing style as appropriate for a man of honor and respect. Because my style is a warrior dance, I share with the clients that as men they must carry themselves as warriors. Warriors stand up and protect their families and their communities. The clients are not permitted to dance at Powwows because when they are involved in drugs and alcohol, they are not examples of warriors and have become a disgrace to their people. They are taught that a warrior is a person of honor, respect, and a symbol of the strength of their family and tribe.

There is one exception when the clients are permitted to dance in a Powwow during their recoveries. In January, the BICO ministry holds a traditional Powwow for the community. It is called the Overcomers Sobriety Powwow and is held in celebration of an alcohol and drug-free lifestyle. At this event the clients can take part by singing with the drum and are allowed to dance when the Master of Ceremonies (MC) calls for an 'Intertribal' dance. During an Intertribal dance everyone can dance and regalia is not required, so the clients can dance in jeans. This gives them an opportunity to see the pride and respect afforded to the dancers as they participate in the event. It is our hope at Overcomers that the clients gain a sense of pride, a positive self-image, and self-esteem.

At Wiconi Family Camp in Turner, Oregon, we hold a Powwow on the Saturday of the four-day annual gathering starting at noon and continuing until 10.00 pm. Our Powwow dancers are mostly made up of the camp attendees, the majority of whom are Christian. Our event draws over six hundred people, and has become popular with the local community. The dancers who participate in the Powwow come from several tribes. Some dance in the style of their particular Northwest tribe, but in the Powwow world there are several dance styles that have taken on a pan-tribal appeal and others dance in these styles as well. These pan-tribal dances are mostly representative of the Northern plains and Woodland tribes, and it is acceptable for people other than members of these tribes to dance these styles. The Wiconi campers come from several Christian denominations, and obviously, they choose to attend. At the Overcomers program, some men attend voluntarily, some are court-ordered, and others are highly encouraged to attend by their families or their parole officers.

Becoming a dancer in the Powwow world has its own Rite of Passage. When my family and I first considered dancing at the Powwow, we knew and (also learned more of) the many details and protocols that exist to become dancers. In the Native world there is no division between the secular and the sacred world – or between religion and the Native spiritual world. Becoming a dancer means setting out on a journey down a sacred path. In the contextual world, the dancer's journey becomes a seamless blend of the Christian and Native traditional worlds.

We began with the desire to dance, and this was followed by a time of prayer, not to some obscure god, but to Jesus Christ. It became a family matter, which led to the desire for all members to start out on the path toward becoming dancers. A dance style had to be chosen for each person, and that selection included the protocol of seeking out a mentor who could be your teacher and guide on this journey. There are four major dance styles for men to choose from: Men's Traditional, Grass Dancer, Chicken, and Fancy. The women may select from: Women's Traditional, Jingle Dress, and Fancy Shawl. Now comes the selection of designs and colors or the regalia to go with your dance style. If you want to use eagle feathers, you have to go through the process of ordering an eagle from the Department of Fish and Wildlife. Because my style requires an eagle for parts of my regalia, I had to wait until I had all the feathers necessary for my style of dance. It can take up to four years to receive them and the permit required to carry them. Once all the preparation is completed, the actual ceremony – a Rite of Passage – takes place at the Powwow circle. All of the above-mentioned preparations make up the Entering and Liminal Phases of a Rite of Passage.

I know these do not describe all the Powwow dance styles and all that is involved completely; I mention them only to show the amount of preparation required just to understand one aspect of my Native culture and the amount of critical contextualization that must take place. This is best done from an insider's view and not from an educated person from another cultural background. The comparison between the Overcomers program and Wiconi Family Camp shows that when these areas of our cultural world are allowed to become a part of our Christian world, change and transition take place and ceremony occurs during the Liminal Phase. The lives of the participants are changed, resulting in a more positive view of who they are as Native people. The staff at both programs see the benefits of incorporating dancing into Native Christian lives.

Singing with the Drum

Since the beginning of time, singing along with the drum has been a natural part of the Native American world. Today there are numerous drum groups across the country singing songs new and old. Some of the new songs have arisen as a result of the Native American contextual ministry movement. This movement has inspired several musical groups to create songs specifically for use with the Native drum in Christian worship. Native musicians like Robert Soto from Texas and Jonathan Maracle of Canada have composed many of the drum songs that are now some of the standards we use today. These singers have inspired many other newer groups who are now creating even more new drum songs. These songs are unique in that they use the familiar rhythmic beat of traditional drum songs combined with Christian lyrics. These songs can take the form of what are called 'straight' songs or 'word' songs. Straight songs use only vocables[3] and chanting with traditional Native rhythms. Word songs are sung with lyrics either in English or the languages of Native people. Contextual word songs have the same traditional rhythmic beat, but the songs incorporate Christian lyrics set to traditional or contemporary tunes.

The Overcomers staff have become very comfortable using these types of drum songs, and view them as an important part of the recovery program's approach. During the interview process for clients to get into the Overcomers program, they are made aware of the program's requirements and style of ministry. The incorporation of the drum with recovery programs is not new, but the drum songs used during the Overcomers program are unique because they use contextual songs with Christian lyrics. They use both word and straight songs. One of the favorite songs the cli-

---

[3] Syllables without a specific meaning.

ents enjoy singing is called 'Jesus is Lord'.[4] Each singer gets a chance to say the words 'Jesus is Lord' as the lead verse to the song. Another of the clients' favorite songs comes from Rev. 22.1, where John shares his vision of a river flowing from the throne of God. Fittingly the song is called 'The River of Life'. Music can be a powerful medium for the expression of biblical truth and Christian theology, and the songs used by the Overcomers are no exception. The main difference from Family Camp is that the Overcomers clients have never heard the songs before. At Family Camp, many are familiar with the contextual songs and sing as part of the opening call to worship and also at the Powwow held on Saturday. In either case the singers and the listeners are edified and God is glorified.

Because the songs are new to the Overcomers clients, they learn each word and its meaning while singing the songs to the drum beat. Not all people are gifted with rhythm. Some of the men pick up the beat right away and others never do, but all participate in the learning time. The time the clients spend around the drum creates close relationships with the staff and each other. The singing with the drum has been used by God in special ways to help these Native clients break free from the destructive hold alcohol has over them. The Overcomers program sees more than 70% of their clients start a new life free of alcohol – a strikingly high success rate.

The healing and the sense of awe the drum songs instill in both the Overcomers and Family Camp staff show them the contribution the drum makes in their overall change and transition. This also occurs in the clients as their lives are forever transformed. The Family Camp attendees learn that the drum can be used as a God-glorifying instrument. With this new view, the songs can lead the people into a worship experience unlike any they have ever seen or had the opportunity to experience. In either case, the sacred time created by the use of the drum and the songs sung is just another factor that contributes to the Rite of Passage theme present at the Brethren in Christ program and Wiconi Family Camp. Staff at both venues see that worship with the use of a

---

[4] The songs mentioned in this section were written and produced by Jonathan Maracle of Broken Walls, www.brokenwalls.com.

drum is an innovation if people have never worshiped that way before.

The Smudging Ritual

I started my contextual journey with the Smudging Ritual over twenty-five years ago. I had lived in two worlds most of my life – half in the Christian church world and half in my Native traditional world. As a young man, I was not allowed to be Native in the Church, and as a Christian, I was not completely welcome in my Native world. It was during these years when I started wondering why there had to be such a big disconnect between the two worlds. I began to study scripture from the viewpoint of my Native American world view. Without doing that, I could only see biblical Hebrew through the eyes of theology given me by a Western, white-dominated view of scripture.

I entered a whole new contextual world that was not popular at the time. It was like stepping away from the King James Version of the Bible and daring to read other versions. What I discovered was that the biblical Hebrew people were much like our Native American people. I could relate to their natural, 'earthy' way of approaching God. Their world was the root of our Christian heritage, and they set in place much of how we now relate to God. Many of the ways they chose to worship are not used in today's church, but some are. Priestly traditions and worshiping God in the tabernacle in the wilderness progressed to worship in the grand temple made of stone and precious metals. There are other ways of worship that are no longer used, such as sacrificing animals by draining their blood and then burning that animal on an altar. The ritual of sending smoke up to heaven as a pleasing aroma in God's nostrils is noted widely in scripture, as is the burning of incense. Incense burned to God most High was honored by God and the burning of incense to other gods was displeasing to Him.

Smudging (burning of incense) is a Native ritual used for blessings, purification, and prayers to bless a person or object. This ritual is used both at Overcomers and at Wiconi Family Camp. When the sweat lodges are built in each program, the ground and the structure are blessed and prayed over with the act of smudging. Smudging is done by fanning the smoldering smoke given off by burning various herbs held inside an abalone shell. Other containers are sometimes used, or the herbs are burned as a bundle or in braided form without a container. The herbs used most commonly are sage, sweet grass, cedar, and tobacco. There are other herbs but these are the most widely used among the Native American tribes of North America.

In biblical days, the Hebrew people used incenses such as frankincense and myrrh and mixtures made specifically for burning. There was a special incense used in the Holy of Holies to 'smudge' the Ark of the Covenant and the Mercy Seat. The incense came from the Altar of Incense which was outside the veil separating the Holy Place from the Holy of Holies. In Lk. 1.8-10, Zechariah, the father of John the Baptist, was chosen by his division of priests to go into the temple of the Lord to burn incense in the Holy of Holies. Similarly in the Native world, to be selected to burn incense (smudging) in a ceremony is a special privilege. In Exod. 30.34-36, a recipe for the making of incense is given, 'Then the Lord said to Moses, take fragrant spices – gum resin, onycha and galbanum – and pure frankincense, all in equal amounts and make a blend of incense, the work of a perfumer'. Native Americans use incense just as the Hebrew people did.

The Smudging Ritual is offered to the clients at Overcomers and the attendees at Family Camp. A smudging can be done for a group or individually. When it is done as a group, the person conducting the ritual may stand in front of or in the center of the group. Each person is fanned individually with the smoke from head to toe and the leader may even have the person turn around. As a Christian and a practitioner of Native American rituals, I can see that Smudging Rituals reflect a Rite of Passage theme. As a sacred ritual, the smudgings are conducted to begin and end many ceremonies. The time frame between these smudgings may be seen as a Liminal Phase. Ceremony takes place during the Liminal Phase and is the place where change and transition can happen. Much can be learned during the Liminal Phase. For the Overcomers clients this ritual is considered a sacred time and promotes healing.

Table 1
The Influence of Ritual for Participants in the BICO
Program and Wiconi Family Camp (WFC)

Rituals	Liminal Experience	Learning	Innovation
Sweat Lodge	BICO – As you enter, prayer & purification. WFC – participation in a prayer ritual.	BICO – presence of God felt in the lodge. WFC– not as scary as previously thought.	This ritual can be performed contextually as a new ritual I can use in my Christian walk.
Pipe Ritual & Bundle	BICO – Pipe Ceremony is very sacred to clients. WFC – sacred because of its historical use.	BICO – contextual usage of rituals. WFC– understanding the use of rituals.	Rituals once seen as too traditional are now given Christ–honoring meanings.
Powwow Dance	WFC – Move from structure to freedom of expression by the dancers.	WFC– dance styles and meanings are realized & adapted in a contextual manner.	Christians can Powwow dance, opening a new dimension of freedom and obedience to Christ.
Singing with Drum	BICO – participation and community in singing. WFC– call to worship, sense of entering sacred space.	BICO – learn and sing drum songs. WFC– A sense of awe and respect for the ceremony.	Drums can be used and seen as good and healing – not bad as they have been told.
Smudging Ritual	BICO – used to enter a sacred time and space. WFC – experience a sense of reverence.	BICO – ritual is part of clients' recovery. WFC – remove negative thoughts.	A traditional ritual may now be understood as sacred and part of their healing process.

Experiencing these rituals encourages innovation and the further exploration of contextualization. Many of the people at Overcomers and Family Camp have heard of and even seen the

Smudging Ritual performed, but it is the use of the ritual as a contextual expression of Christian faith that makes it intensely meaningful. There are similarities between the usages of the Smudging Ritual in these two programs. The Overcomers clients sense the sacred aspects of the ritual. They have experienced smudging in the traditional Native life, and now they are experiencing this sacred Smudging Ritual in the context of a Christian treatment program. They are set free to experience a new form of expression of their Christian faith – one which was denied them because the fear of using a pagan ritual might be dishonoring to God. As Family Camp attendees see and take part in the ritual for the very first time, they experience a sense of awe. Negative thoughts about the ritual disappear, and there is a realization that they can participate in the ritual in their personal lives as well. Knowledge gained in the Liminal Phase in the Native American world is sacred time and considered part of the ceremony.

Conclusion

The Rites of Passage theme has emerged as central to my understanding of the success of both the Overcomers program and Family Camp. In both programs the Sweat Lodge Ceremony can lead to change and transition in a person's life and be a profound turning point in their spiritual growth as a disciple of Christ.

As a liminal experience, the Sweat Lodge Ceremony includes both the act of purification through smudging before entry and the use of steam when inside. Purification takes place both physically and spiritually. The participants are prepared for the event with an educational talk before entering and again while inside the lodge. Learning new information while in the Liminal Phase is one of the aspects of a Rites of Passage ceremony.

Past attempts at the removal of their culture caused many problems for today's Native Americans. The ministry paradigm designed to change their way of life had many faults. They had been taught by Native and non-Native church leaders alike that their cultural expressions were bad and demonic and needed to be rejected. Now we have contextualization – not a theory, not a dream, but an actual approach to Native ministry that opens doors to the boldness and freedom to be both fully Native and Christian. Contextual ministry did not just 'happen' – it had to start at some point with a vision to see change. These concepts spent many years in liminality and emerged to reintegrate leaders' and followers' untapped potential and opportunities.

Becoming contextual has often demanded that we question some of our previous Christian teaching. To tell someone to step away from a non-contextual church, that some of the ways of the Western church are wrong, and to tell missionaries that in the name of love they may have been doing damage to our Native communities – closed many relational doors.[5] The move from non-contextual to contextual was a challenging process and a Rite of Passage the BICO staff and participants have had to enter, learn, and implement for these programs to work successfully. The BICO program and Wiconi Family Camp have both accepted the challenge to create contextual expressions of faith that blend the Native traditional and Christian worlds in appropriate ways. These two ministries are leading the way for many others to travel. Now that many of the barriers have been removed, change is an open door for even more innovation. Programs like these are the forerunners of many more ministries that will build on what we have begun and take contextual ministry into the future. This has been my hope and calling from the very beginning.

---

[5] Ronald A. Heifetz and Marty Linsky *Leadership on the Line: Staying Alive Through the Dangers of Leading* (Boston, MA: Harvard Business Review Press, 2013), p. 93.

7

THE LIMINAL PHASE OF TRANSITION IN RITES OF PASSAGE: THE BICO ALCOHOL TREATMENT PROGRAM

To take the courage to enter the change process is to believe you are going to come out on the other end as a different person. We all want to believe there will be changes that will affect not only our own life but the lives of many others.

Some common examples of significant changes people go through would include: being born, becoming a teenager, getting a driver's license, graduating from high school, accepting a first steady job, entering college and then graduating, joining the military, getting married, and having children. Many Native Americans navigate changes using their tribal rituals and ceremonies. Some of these include: puberty rituals, naming ceremonies, receiving an eagle feather, becoming a Powwow dancer, and going on a vision quest.

The Liminal Phase

Some of the changes or chapters in my life came easily, but others required *enormous* effort. One of the most challenging times of change and transition in my life took place at United States Marine Corps Recruit Training (boot camp). Before joining the Marines, I had come to a point in my life where I was ready for significant change. I had been working as a maintenance mechanic at a local clock company in Michigan, and I knew this was not the future I was looking for. I was ambitious, wanted more for my life, and decided to become one of 'The Few, the Proud, the Marines'. Historically, in my Native world becoming a warrior was a life stage in the process of becoming a man. Although this tradition was once significant in my culture, it has lost its previous level of importance. Still, deep inside me was the desire to accept the challenge and become a warrior – and boot camp was my ritual/ceremony toward becoming a man. Marine Corps boot camp is an excellent example of the Liminal Phase. In this time of transition you decide to enter (The Entering Phase), you spend twelve weeks in training (The Liminal Phase), and you then exit with a graduation 'ceremony' (The Reintegration Phase). You enter as a boy and exit as a warrior. All the characteristics of Rites of Passage are present in the boot camp experience.

I have experienced many changes, as have we all. The latest chapter of my life – a time of serious change and transition – is the result of leaving my employment as a carpenter and joining the Wiconi International staff as Director.

Organizations go through changes (chapters) as well. The Brethren in Christ Mission had to make some critical changes in order to get where they are today. Some were very challenging and some came quite easily. One major Rite of Passage journey Overcomers had to go through in order to have a high success rate was to embrace boldly while maintaining an attitude of humility.

Some ministries, churches, and secular treatment programs can have an almost arrogant attitude toward the *correctness* of their methods and leadership styles. We have all seen examples of this type of behavior. 'The illusion that seduces all leaders and followers is that we have the "right form" for God's work, and we trust the form and system rather than God.'[1]

In the ministry world Richard Twiss negotiated for years, there were difficult challenges to overcome. There were a few obstinate individuals who opposed contextual ministry because their views conflicted with his. Closely related was the belief that their current methods were the 'right and the only way to do ministry'. This can

---

[1] Lingenfelter, *Leading Cross-Culturally*, p. 101.

be compared with the attitude that we see when some people strongly believe only one version of the Bible is correct for church use.

'Hanging onto outdated ministry and religious traditions because of the meanings they used to provide can be a morbid practice.'[2] The Hebrew people had to let go of the influences of Egypt before they could cross over into the Promised Land. The Navajo Brethren in Christ Mission staff and leadership had to let go of the strong influence of their past denominational liturgy and ministry methods. They were looking for ways that would better reach and help Native Americans to accept the gospel and bring men out of alcoholism. They realized the older methods were still not producing adequate results.

Liminality and Contextualization

All of the above-mentioned cases and situations required going through a process of an Entering Phase, a Liminal Phase, then followed by a Reaggregation (Reintegration) Phase back into the world. To become a contextual ministry church or program requires the development of an understanding of different methods. Darrell Whiteman says,

> Contextualization means to develop a unique, locally-informed cultural expression of the gospel. The result will be that the gospel itself will be understood in ways the universal church has neither experienced nor understood before. This expands the wider church's understanding of the kingdom of the Creator.[3]

When these types of expressions are approved for experimentation and then implementation, it takes time to process the changes before they are considered 'normal' methods. But it is not only about the actions we take, but also what we can do to affect the spiritual development of individuals. Native minister Craig Smith (of the Christian and Missionary Alliance Church) in his book,

---

[2] Nelson and Appel, *How to Change Your Church*, p. 65.
[3] Darrell L. Whiteman, *Anthropology and Mission: The Incarnational Connection* (Chicago, IL: CCGM Publishing, 2003), pp. 2-4.

Whiteman's Gospel, states, 'I believe the best person to decide how a traditional person conforms his life to biblical principles is the traditionalist himself under the guidance of the Holy Spirit'.[4]

Contrary to Smith's view, I believe it is the Christian Indigenous innovator and not the traditional person who can best make the decisions to use contextual approaches. The traditionalist is usually not biblically-knowledgeable, while the Christian Indigenous innovator *who is* can make the best adaptations. In many ways making change in this Liminal Phase hinges on one's commitment to the cause. In the liminal time of a Rites of Passage journey, the door to experimentation opens up. It was my experience that in this phase I felt a strong desire to be creative and experiment with many possible ways to contextualize. Sometimes this would mean speaking directly to the issues, not only through my personal ministry approach, but also to many who were just coming into the realization of the legitimate usage of contextual methods in their own ministries.

New 'realizers' go through a process of understanding how to 'do' critical contextualization. I explored many possibilities and was usually working on more than one at the same time in order to find those that worked best. When experimenting with a Potawatomi ritual or ceremony, I was also thinking how that approach might work in another Native tribe's cultural setting and context. It takes a special type of person to work through the Rites of Passage process. It takes someone who has the vision well established in their personal makeup and has the need to see the development of processes that can lead to change. Rick Richardson comments in *Evangelism Outside the Box*, 'There is certainly a need for prophets who call us back to the ancient ways. But there is also a great need for evangelists who will translate core values into new practices that will resonate with and reach pre-Christian people.'[5]

You Cannot Not Change
Nelson and Appel give the following definition of change in *How to Change Your Church (Without Killing It)*: 'The word change means to cause to turn or pass from one state to another, to vary in form

---

[4] Craig Stephen Smith and Bill McCartney, *Whiteman's Gospel* (Winnipeg, Manitoba, Canada: Intertribal Christian Communications, 1998), p. 126.

[5] Richardson, *Evangelism Outside the Box*, p. 25.

or essence; to alter or make different'.[6] Our Native ancestors realized this and developed rituals to show people a way to move from one stage to another. So whether the change is dealing with a person's age, a puberty rite, a social status change, or even the transition to the world of the dead, there was a way to cope with change through ceremony.

At Overcomers the aim is to work with Native men who are trapped within the throes of alcohol and drug addiction. As a Rite of Passage ceremony, they must start the program by entering a re-learning stage in the Liminal Phase. This prepares them for an ending or Reaggregation Phase (reintegration) into society as individuals who have completed this Rite of Passage ceremony and can now live at a *new level* in society without experiencing addiction problems.

These individuals have made a break with the default setting that alcohol and drugs have produced by going through the Rite of Passage journey of the Overcomers program. Through years of usage, day-by-day defaults are established and require a deprogramming time at the Brethren in Christ ministry. 'Changing behavior at the level of default settings requires new insight and ongoing practice, practice, practice.'[7] I list in Table 2 the key parts of the Overcomers program, including the various ceremonies.

Changing habits or default settings transforms the picture of reality that lies in the mind of the individual. This current image of reality controls their lives. What the Navajo BICO program does is help the clients envision a life *without* drugs and alcohol through the influence of new ideas or 'innovations'. These new ways may have been known but never developed, or lost from view because of their previous lifestyles.

---

[6] Nelson and Appel, *How to Change Your Church*, p. xiv.
[7] Sharon D. Parks, *Leadership Can Be Taught: A Bold Approach for a Complex World* (Boston, MA: Harvard Business Review Press, 2013), p. 86.

Table 2
Structure of the Rite of Passage at the
BICO Alcohol Treatment Program

SEPARATION/ENTERING PHASE: Clients are interviewed for entry into the Brethren in Christ Overcomers program. Entry into the program is held in the middle of the desert away from friends and family. The program has rules: Use of drugs or alcohol is prohibited.
LIMINAL PHASE: They start with the realization that life as they knew it has now changed. Their bodies start to go through changes, and they start to eat regular meals. Classes begin in Bible study, computer skills, finance, and relationships. Innovations are made using new information. Prayers are said in the contextual way; plans are made for the Sweat Lodge Ceremony. Clients observe the Christian lifestyles of the staff members. Clients attend the Mission's church service on Sunday afternoons. Field trips are taken to cultural sites, and visits are made to local churches.
REAGGREGATION/REINTEGRATION PHASE: One week prior to graduation, one last Sweat Lodge Ceremony is held. A special Pipe Ceremony is conducted to bless the clients. Family and friends attend the graduation. Clients prepare to leave and step back into their communities as new creations.

The Change Solution Lies in the People

The mental picture of this reality is in the people, and the remedy is to change that picture and give the clients another one. The method used by the Overcomers program seems to work, as they view the clients in the following manner: 'Because the problem lies in people, the solution lies in them, too. So the work of addressing an adaptive challenge must be done by the people connected to the problem.'[8] A medicine man or shaman treats people by focusing on their issues, not just their symptoms. Much of modern medicine concentrates on the symptoms of a problem,

---

[8] Heifetz, Linsky, and Grashow, *The Practice of Adaptive Leadership*, p. 74.

but it is more effective to work with the person in this psychological 'no-man's land' between the old reality and the new one. There is a place of limbo between the old sense of identity and the new. It's the time when the old ways of living (or doing things) are gone but the new ways do not feel comfortable yet. It's a time when it is not clear who you are or what is real.

To Enter the Liminal Door

Within transition, change, and re-imaging life remains the question of a client's desire to make the change, even with the longing to continue to drink looming over him. At various points in the program, the true desire to change their picture of reality is tapped into and can be a continual motivation for him to redeem his life. When this happens it is an awakening and visualizing of a door toward finding direction in this life's journey. Some never realize this and never make the break with alcohol. Those who had gone into transition unwillingly or unwittingly find it very hard to admit that a new beginning and a new phase of their lives might be at hand or even be possible.[9]

It is in this environment that knowledge that may have once been seen as healthy and good is reintroduced to the clients, and an awakening takes place within those who overcome addiction. This is what innovation is all about. It is not some grandiose idea never known before, such as the invention of the wheel. It can be basic ideas explained as innovation; this new awareness affects the entire group in the program. The clients at Navajo BICO are living examples of just such a social system.

---

[9] Bridges, *Transitions: Making Sense of Life's Changes*, p. 9.

CHAPTER 8

CURRENT REALITIES AND ADAPTIVE WORK FOR THE FUTURE: FEAR VERSUS THE FAITH TO STEP INTO THE UNKNOWN

My personal approach to creating change in this paradigm of contextual ministry has been to step out boldly and create new methods and styles of ministry. I did not know whether this was the right way to proceed or not, but I did know we had to do something – and that whatever we did should be treated as an experiment. This approach is an example of Everett Rogers' 'Diffusion of Innovations' theory: 'Diffusion has a special character because of the newness of the idea in the message content. Thus some degree of uncertainty and perceived risk is involved in the diffusion process.'[1]

Leadership development does not happen overnight, although your leadership position can almost come that quickly. We indeed went through a transitional period in the Native American contextual movement. We began with no script, no examples, and no leaders. Those of us determined enough to break with older models of ministry practices chose to walk a new road we believed was better. I battled with the fear of stepping into full-time ministry leadership for a while before I made the decision to do it. But with Lora's encouragement, I did choose to make the move and now I have the opportunity to create a 'new' Wiconi.

---

[1] Rogers, *Diffusion of Innovations*, p. 35.

God has moved me down the road of contextual ministry – opening doors and creating opportunities – despite my fears. Fear about embarking into contextual ministry does not just affect those involved in it, but also those on the margins – non-contextual ministers who are watching and weighing the pros and cons before making the move to get on board. 'The question of risk lies at the root of our fears. Fear is always a significant obstacle to a life of Christian pilgrimage. Once we identify our fears, we may then deal with them through the application of truth and the contextual understanding of scripture.'[2]

For years I was in a transitional phase, always feeling as if I were betwixt and between. I entered the 'world' of contextual transition as a leader, although I was unaware there were others across the country also doing this kind of ministry. In our region (the Southwest), I took a group of people through the process of change, transition, and liminality until we created an active contextual Native American ministry. Regarding this process Bridges notes, 'It was not the image of the land of milk and honey that got the people out of Egypt or through the wilderness to the Promised Land – it was Moses' skill as a transition leader'.[3]

Our skills in leading people through transition happened at the grass-roots level. I had to attempt to explain what contextual ministry was to several major opinion leaders in the community. I also wanted to change how they viewed our church plant. Rogers defines opinion leadership as:

> … the degree to which an individual is able to influence informally other individual's attitudes or overt behaviors in a desired way with relative frequency. A change agent is an individual who attempts to influence clients' innovation-decisions in a direction that is deemed desirable by a change agency.[4]

Diffusion of Innovation in Native Ministries

To influence a culture it is necessary to bring about change either positively or negatively. In our movement we believe the contextu-

---

[2] Lingenfelter, *Transforming Culture*, p. 61.
[3] Bridges, *Managing Transitions: Making the Most of Change*, p. 65.
[4] Rogers, *Diffusion of Innovations*, p. 38.

al approaches we are using influence positive change. To accomplish this type of change – whether in our Native American culture or in any other – cultural insiders are absolutely necessary. This is because 'without this person there will not be genuine contextualization, but only surface-level adaptations'.[5] We are bringing about innovation – not adaptation – to the Native ministry world. Rogers writes, 'Diffusion is a special type of communication concerned with the spread of messages that are perceived as new ideas'.[6] Stepping out to introduce innovation in a new context requires a very creative mind. I have been able to apply Rogers' Diffusion of Innovations theory to the Native American contextualization movement and also to the recovery approach at the BICO Alcohol Treatment Program.

The treatment program has introduced new ideas and ways of living to the clients so they can change the image of a life they can have. They may have been aware of some of the new ideas as innovation, but lacked the training to apply them *practically* to their lives as the contextual model has done. The new ideas (innovations) the men in recovery discover and apply to create change during the transition time are such things as: a better work ethic, positive relationship building, money management, child-raising, and Christian biblical understanding. These new ways of living are taught throughout the three-month program and seem to make a difference in their successful recovery from drugs and alcohol. Rogers says,

> Simply to regard the adoption of innovation as rational (defined as use of the most effective means to reach a given end) and to classify rejection as stupid is to fail to understand that individual innovation-decisions are idiosyncratic. They are based on an individual's perception of the innovation. Whether considered right or wrong by scientific experts who seek to evaluate an innovation objectively, adoption or rejection is always 'right' in the eyes of the individual who made the innovation-decision (at least at the time the decision is made).[7]

---

[5] Twiss, 'Rescuing Theology from the Cowboys', p. 113.
[6] Rogers, *Diffusion of Innovations*, p. 35.
[7] Rogers, *Diffusion of Innovations*, p. 116.

Contextual ministry is not usually considered an option by seminary students trained in the Western style. Yet some people seem to understand the concepts well – especially those who are cultural insiders. The majority of clients at the BICO program are Native, and since the program is located in New Mexico, mostly Navajo. Treatment program methods and approaches end with the clients having the opportunity to make a personal decision for Christ, thus leading to recovery. The approach at Overcomers is geared for this particular region and clientele. 'Since we seldom reflect on our underlying values, we assume everyone thinks like we do, and we imagine that anyone who reasons differently is incompetent, rude or not raised "properly"'.[8] The staff at Overcomers have developed a program that regards the cultural traditions of the men as normal and natural to them. This has made all the difference in their treatment.

The Native American Contextual Movement has met the need to create ministry models *for* Native Americans, *by* Native Americans. There is also a need for the development of Native contextual leadership. Plueddemann recognized this and said, 'It would be absurd to expect that a foreign "expert" could teach a leadership course in Nigeria [or for that matter to Native Americans] without an understanding of the traditional cultural assumptions about how leaders are developed'.[9] I have kept this in mind as my leadership skills grow while working with Wiconi. I have gained knowledge, understanding, and trust from my Native community. The members of a Native community are the ones who bestow the granting of leadership to a person, especially a person from within their own ranks. Lingenfelter shares a quote from Max DePree that says exactly what I believe about leadership: '[It] is how one lives within a structure, respecting the people, accepting their differences, and engaging them in ways that inspire trust and transforms yet sustains relationships and structure'.[10]

---

[8] Plueddemann, *Leading Across Cultures*, p. 64.
[9] Plueddemann, *Leading Across Cultures*, p. 204.
[10] Lingenfelter, *Leading Cross-Culturally*, p. 99.

Agents of Innovation and Change

Innovators and change agents live in the Liminal Phase most of the time. Most ministries are not aware that other ways of doing ministry even exist. Visioning, dreaming, being bold enough to change, and being creative is where the Liminal Phase does its best work. Seeing a glimpse of a 'preferred future' – as Richard Twiss would say – is the key to bringing our Native American people closer to Jesus Christ. Liminality and creativity go hand in hand. Transition and change happen as leaders buck the system and open the door for innovation to take root and grow. But there are too few of these creative leaders – their tribe must increase. 'It means thinking outside the box and coloring outside the lines. It means daring to look around and envision what lies ahead. Is there a newer, more efficient method?'[11]

Something Richard Twiss said explains my own personal journey: 'As I look back on that time, I realize I was starting down the road of an internal, personal, decolonization process and deconstruction of my conservative evangelical Christian philosophical introduction to biblical faith'.[12] I too began to challenge my previously-learned ideals and values concerning typical approaches to 'doing church'. I had been indoctrinated into a method of maintaining, when I so wanted to change the way ministry was being done. I wanted Native American nonbelievers to have culturally-appropriate opportunities to meet Christ. From the very start, my calling has been making the gospel more easily accessible to Native Americans by creating an approach that looks different from the Western model.

Successful ministry to Native people does not mean creating more Western-style churches. But as Paul says, 'I have become all things to all people that I might save some' (1 Cor. 9.22). My ultimate purpose is 'To know Christ and make him known'.[13] That means in our Native American world we must create innovative

---

[11] Samuel R. Chand and Cecil B. Murphey, *Futuring: Leading Your Church into Tomorrow* (Grand Rapids, MI: Baker Books, 2002), p. 123.

[12] Twiss, 'Rescuing Theology from the Cowboys', p. 60.

[13] C. Wayne Mayhall, 'Effective Evangelism: To Know Christ and to Make Him Known', *Christian Research Institute* 31.4 (2008): Title page.

ways of presenting Jesus to Native people – while at the same time removing barriers to the task.

The process of change and transition I have had to go through to get to where I am today has been a journey of patience: patience with myself, patience with others around me, and patience with those opposed to my ministry's direction. Finally, the road did smooth out and progressed from two-track, to gravel, to pavement, and then to a highway. It has taken a long time. Today I look back on how, at the beginning, as we created a contextual ministry, there was a feeling of being normal, natural, and Indigenous. It felt like being gone for a long time and finally coming home. It was a journey of self-discovery, trying to find a fit for my Potawatomi culture and tradition within my faith in Jesus – a faith that was so heavily meshed with Western Christian expression that there was no room to move.

In taking this contextual position, were there many obstacles that had an impact and hindered my leadership development? There were, as Heifetz *et al.*, describe: 'Loyalties to people who may not believe you are doing the right thing; fear of incompetence; uncertainty about taking the right path; fear of loss; [and] not having the stomach for the hard part of the journey'.[14] I felt like my biggest personal failure was not trusting God completely.

When I first entered ministry (part-time), I trusted like a young child does. As time went on, and the waves began to get bigger and the wind began to blow, the concerns of family life filled my mind. Bills had to be paid: school tuition, rent, car payments, groceries, and insurance – all these kept me from jumping into full-time ministry. I like the metaphor Bridges uses for managing transition. He says it's like learning to swim – letting go of the edge and just swimming.

> You may have heard the swimming teacher say, at such a time, 'I won't let you sink.' Without trust in the teacher, the step toward independence and the mastery of a new skill is less likely to happen. At that moment with fear balanced against hope, it is trust that makes the difference.[15]

---

[14] Heifetz, Linsky, and Grashow, *The Practice of Adaptive Leadership*, p. 247.
[15] Bridges, *Managing Transitions: Making the Most of Change*, p. 108.

I had to trust the teacher – Jesus Christ. All of this was truly the story of my ministry journey in the liminal time – the journey to becoming an effective leader. By sharing honestly, I want people to know that I am just a common man, pitiful in every way in comparison to my Creator. And being aware of my shortcomings and failures will help me become the servant God is making me. Psalm 139.23-24 says it best: 'Search me, O God, and know my heart; try me and know my concerns, and see if there is any rebellious way in me, and lead me in the ancient way'.[16]

---

[16] *Holy Bible, Modern English Version* (Lake Mary, FL: Charisma House, 2014).

CONCLUSION

WICONI IN TRANSITION: THE PROCESS OF LIMINALITY

These examples of change, transition, and liminality offer a way of understanding my personal journey into leadership in the Wiconi ministry and also the changes in the Wiconi organization. Liminality aptly describes the current position of Wiconi and my place in it. In many respects what we are encountering are rituals and ceremonies parallel to my personal and community life as a Potawatomi Native. Liminality is characterized by a sense of not fitting in totally in any one location. The loss of Richard Twiss, the transition and change of the Wiconi organization, and leaving my secular employment all play a part in this ceremony. Hiebert and Shaw have described a situation such as mine played out in people's lives in Native rituals throughout the world. They say, 'They lose their status in normal society, and enter a state of transition – a time during which they are in the cracks between two identities: neither here nor there, no longer the old but not yet the new'.[1] Yes, this is right where I am, but the reassuring thought is this – it is a normal position to be in. The Liminal Phase happens, it happens every new day, and it will continue to happen in the lives of all people everywhere. It's like changing gears in a standard shift automobile. You have the metaphorical keys to start the 'vehicle' of an idea/method/approach to doing something. You put the keys in and start the process. You run it in first gear for a

---

[1] Hiebert and Shaw, *Understanding Folk Religion*, p. 297.

time until you get to a point when you need to change. Then you grab the shifter, depress the clutch, and move from first gear to neutral. Neutral is the position between changes, and it is necessary to start there in order to move to another gear. Most cultures or languages do not even have a name for it.

Managing changes and transitions during the Liminal Phase (or neutral zone) is where my artistic experience is most helpful. As a potter, I understand the process of creating change. I take a lump of clay, handle it with controlled force, and with gentle persuasion I begin to shape the clay through several stages needed toward an end product that becomes a piece of emerging art. In *Leadership Can Be Taught*, Sharon Parks explains this as:

> ... a practice of leadership that is less like command and control and more like artistry. What they are practicing in both theory building and case-in-point teaching, is best understood as akin to processes of creativity – evoking innovation and more adequate way of seeing ... in a time of extraordinary cultural change.[2]

There is a reason my ancestors created Rites of Passage ceremonies. They knew the importance of rituals. I have always had to *bend* to the cultural ways of the West in order to navigate and survive within a different culture. By claiming the authenticity of who I am as a Native person, I can even – in a Western way – begin to see my cultural understanding as a legitimate way of expressing myself without feeling that I am odd, wrong, or even backward. Using the familiar rituals of my world can show us all how to live more balanced lives. Roberta King highlights the importance of Native rituals and customs saying, 'Expressions that were used included "teaching that goes to the depths of our hearts," "counsel," "advise," "show the way we should walk," and "teach us new things that we have not yet learned"'.[3] Living in two worlds created a growing unrest in my soul. The dualistic style of Western Christianity created a gap in my life that was filled when I began walking in my Native cultural ways.

---

[2] Parks, *Leadership Can Be Taught*, p. 208.
[3] Roberta R. King, *Pathways in Christian Music Communication: The Case of the Senufo of Cote D'Ivoire* (Eugene, OR: Pickwick Publications, 2009), p. 182.

This internal tension was shaped by living in a world with a history of the following attitudes, as listed by Philip Jenkins:

Early white concepts of Native religion generally ranged from devil worship to mere paganism, from which Indians had to be won to Christ. By the turn of the century, however, new respect for Native religion had arisen among white intellectuals, and anthropologists in particular [and I would add theologians and missiologists].[4]

There is a growing awareness of the need for Indigenous people to embrace their own cultures. As Reggie McNeal writes, 'Culture also serves God's purpose. He uses it to shape the hearts of spiritual leaders. This means that culture can be appreciated and studied for its contributions as a heart-shaping drama in the leader's life story.'[5]

Creating a Team in Liminality

The process of building and growing a team also involves Rites of Passage principles. First you enter the process, then experience a Liminal Phase of relationship-building, then you exit when the team is built and ready to move forward. Creating a team begins with understanding the process.

Developing a team requires patience and sensitivity, especially during organizational change and transition. In this new season, I believe we should 'Go for it! Be strong, dream new dreams, honor the past, but do not live there. God has too much in store for us in the Promised Lands He has prepared for our ministry.'[6] But it's up to us to decide to go forward. The past was full of great moments, but those times contain shadows of the low periods as well. I was a part of many of these positive ministry times. While in the Liminal Phase of team building, it is important never to denigrate the past.

---

[4] Philip Jenkins, *Dream Catchers: How Mainstream America Discovered Native Spirituality* (New York: Oxford University Press, 2004), p. 83.

[5] Reggie McNeal, *A Work of Heart: Understanding How God Shapes Spiritual Leaders,* (San Francisco: Jossey Bass, 2011), p. 73.

[6] Nelson and Appel, *How to Change Your Church*, p. xvii.

Moving through the change and transition stage of liminality reminds me of a story I once heard about a new pastor at a church. He wanted to make changes too fast. He wanted to move the piano to the other side of the platform, so on the next Sunday the congregation found the piano moved. That pastor was freed up to pastor elsewhere! Another pastor was called and wanted to make the same change as well. Sometime later the *first* pastor returned to the church one Sunday, and to his surprise the piano was on the opposite side of the church platform. He asked the new pastor how he had gotten the people to accept the change. He said, 'Every week I moved the piano about an inch toward the other side of the church platform'. Effective change takes time and careful pacing.

Pushing the piano all the way was too much, but taking an inch at a time was too little. When making changes and transitions, one way is to push the limits in the Liminal Phase – this can happen when you need to get some forward motion going. When you push beyond people's comfort zones, you can break a barrier which can then set the stage for change beyond that point because it is now within a new comfort zone.

When studying the change process in my research, it became evident that we take the Overcomers' clients through many changes in order to push them beyond their comfort zones. The Liminal Phase is a time that takes them farther than they have gone before and makes moving forward in recovery more acceptable. The same is true with staff and volunteers in organizations like Wiconi and Overcomers, and for those in leadership. It is important for us to keep in mind that people going through change experience real pain, so we need to make change bearable. The pace of change is critical whether in recovery from addiction or going through organizational or leadership changes.

Leadership for the Liminal Phase of Change

Going through Rites of Passage creates discomfort, and we look for answers to make us better able to face the issues. This is what Richard Twiss saw and others are able to see and do within their contexts. They are people 'called of God' as leaders for the Liminal Phase of change.

These liminal leaders, like a shaman or some other special leader in our Native traditional world, walk in the two worlds of traditional and Christian faith. When transition and change happen in our own world, we often question whether the whole thing is worth it, and grow anxious and frustrated. When change interrupts the balance of our lives, we call on these liminal leaders as sent by the Creator. The operating assumption has been that our spiritual leaders already understand spiritual formation and have applied these disciplines to their own lives. It is a discipline not taught in books, but learned from experience in and from contextual ministry.

The pacing of the change process is very important. When you are leading change you must envision taking people through the 'in-between' zone (Liminal Phase). One must take the time to plant vision *within* key leaders before sharing it with everyone, making the process to the preferred future a deliberate one. A leader must engage people in facing challenges, adjusting their values, changing perspectives, and developing new habits of behavior. All of these and other modifications to an individual or group are needed for a successful transition to take place.

A time of liminality offers many opportunities to create 'missional maps'[7] that can suggest ways ahead for Wiconi – and frame responses to its changed ministry situation. The betwixt and between period has purpose for Native people – it is at the core of our rituals and ceremonies. Many Native traditions have found ways to look at times of transition with optimism. When decisions need to be made, we look to the Creator for answers and guidance. When we have lost our direction, we seek a vision, and when children grow we have Rites of Passage ceremonies called puberty rites. 'This liminal place provides initiates with a chaotic limbo condition of transition "betwixt and between" the clearly defined statuses and roles of childhood and adulthood in their society.'[8] People of all ages need these transitional times. Some are expected

---

[7] Roxburgh, *The Missionary Congregation*, p. 23.

[8] A.H. Mathias Zahniser, *Symbol and Ceremony: Making Disciples Across Cultures* (Federal Way, WA: MARC Publications, 1997), pp. 92-93.

– and we prepare for them with rituals – but in the case of death we seek wisdom from our elders who have dealt with death over the years.

Richard Twiss was a brilliant man. He was aware of his mortality – as we all should be – and considered future generations when he made decisions. We owe a great deal to Richard for having the foresight to build a competent team to carry Wiconi ahead – and to continue his desire to impact the generations to come.

Transition and change to contextual ministry can be difficult to navigate, but the lives of many of my Native brothers and sisters are at stake. Their salvation, spiritual development, and deliverance from bondage of whatever kind is worth the effort – and worth our discomfort. Jesus believed they were worth dying for.

I close with the compelling words of a great Native leader:

Chief Tecumseh

(Shawnee, 1768-1813)

So live your life that the fear of death
can never enter your heart.
Trouble no one about their religion;
respect others in their view,
and demand that they respect yours.

Love your life, perfect your life,
beautify all things in your life.

Seek to make your life long and its purpose
in the service of your people.

Prepare a noble death song for the day
when you go over the great divide.
Always give a word or a sign of salute
when meeting or passing a friend,
even a stranger, when in a lonely place.

Show respect to all people and bow to none.
When you arise in the morning,
give thanks for the food and for the joy of living.

If you see no reason for giving thanks,
the fault lies only in yourself.

Abuse no one and nothing,
for abuse turns the wise ones to fools
and robs the spirit of its vision.

When it comes your time to die,
be not like those whose hearts are filled
with fear of death, so that when their time comes
they weep and pray for a little more time
to live their lives over again in a different way.

Sing your death song
and die like a hero going home.[9]

---

[9] Glenn Welker, 'Chief Tecumseh Shawnee', *Indigenous People*, December 10, 2013, Accessed June 2015, http://www.indigenouspeople.net/tecumseh.htm.

GLOSSARY

Cedar: 'Cedar is one of the most important sacred herbs used by the Lakota and other Native Americans for ceremony. The importance and reason for its use by the Native Americans has been echoed by several unrelated cultures throughout the world. Cedar is for the aid of visions and for helping the body and mind in times of great spiritual anxiety and stress.'[1]

Contextualization: 'In recent days missiologists have settled on the term contextualization to describe this task of understanding, communicating, and expressing our faith in culturally-relevant ways'.[2]

Incense: 'Incense is defined as a material that is burned to produce an odor, usually fragrant, and is also referred to as the perfume or fumigation itself that is produced from the burning of plant and other materials'.[3]

Native American/Native Alaskan/First Nations: Members of any of the aboriginal peoples of the Western hemisphere, especially of North America.

Pipe: One of the central ceremonial objects of many American Indian groups. It is considered a microcosm, its parts and decorative colors and motifs corresponding to the essential parts of the universe. It is smoked in personal prayer as well as at collective rites.

---

[1] Kerry Hughes, *The Incense Bible: Plant Scents That Transcend World Culture, Medicine, and Spirituality* (Philadelphia, PA: Haworth Press, 2001), p. 108

[2] Douglas Hayward, 'The Foundation for Critical Contextualization: Prelimi-nary Considerations for Doing Contextualization Among First Nations Christians', *Journal of North American Institute for Indigenous Theological Studies* 6 (2007), p. 144.

[3] Hughes, *The Incense Bible*, p. 8.

Pipe Ceremony: The use of tobacco and the symbolism of the in-
drawn and ascending smoke is employed as a means of
communication between the spirit world and humans.

Sage: 'Sage is one of the most important sacred herbs used by
Lakota and other Native Americans for ceremonies and
rituals'.[4]

Smudging: 'The smudge is a cleansing or purification ceremony
that cleanses body, soul, and spirit. It is done by lighting
sage, sweet grass, or cedar, and then blowing out the fire
causing it to smoke in a shell. In order to obtain cleansing,
the Native person pulls the smoke onto themselves while
the one burning the sage waves an eagle feather or fan to
move the smoke.'[5]

Spiritual Formation: Dallas Willard defines spiritual formation in
the opening sentence of his article in 'Life in the Spirit' as
the 'transformation of professing Christians into Christ-
likeness'.[6]

Sweat Lodge: A hut, lodge, or cavern heated by steam from water
poured on hot stones and used especially by Native Americans for rituals or therapeutic sweating.

Sweet Grass: 'Sweet grass is historically used as a "medicine" or
ceremony plant by Native Americans, especially the Lakota (Sioux), and also as a basket weaving component. Sweet
grass is a very important plant in Native American culture,
and it is used for prayer and during smudging.'[7]

Syncretism: 'Syncretism simply means taking non-biblical Native
beliefs and practices and mixing them into Christian beliefs and practices so that the resultant system has bor-

---

[4] Hughes, *The Incense Bible*, p. 139.

[5] Corky Alexander, *Native American Pentecost: Praxis, Contextualization, Transformation* (Cleveland, TN: Cherohala Press, 2012), p. 54.

[6] Jeffrey Greenman and George Kalantzis, *Life in the Spirit: Spiritual Formation
in Theological Perspective* (Downers Grove, IL: InterVarsity Press, 2010), p. 45.

[7] Hughes, *The Incense Bible*, p. 135.

rowed from each of the contributing systems but is purely neither'.[8]

Tobacco: 'Of all plants none was more suitable than was tobacco for inducing peace or transporting man's thoughts and prayers to Kitche Manitou (Great Spirit). In the first place tobacco was a gift of the spirit. In the second place tobacco was in the nature of an incense sweet to the taste and fragrant to smell. No other plant is endowed with such qualities.'[9]

---

[8] Terry LeBlanc, 'Culture, Faith and Mission: Creating the Future', *Journal of North American Institute for Indigenous Theological Studies* 1 (2003), p. 153.

[9] Basil Johnston, *Ojibway Heritage* (Toronto, ON, Canada: McClelland & Stewart, 2011), p. 43.

Appendix: Wiconi International History

Richard and Katherine Twiss were led by the Lord and convinced that Native ministry conducted in a Western style had been largely ineffective, and that there must be a better way to reach Native people for Christ. Richard stepped away from thirteen years of pastoring an all-white congregation to found Wiconi (wuh-CHO-nee) International with his wife Katherine. He saw that the majority of Native Americans needed to know Christ by experiencing Him through an appropriate, culturally-relevant approach. Richard and Katherine longed to see contextual change and transition happen. Richard was a gifted leader and was able to motivate others to join his causes.

Many years ago when Richard was pastoring his church, the Lord gave him the vision to create a ministry that would reach Native Americans in a far different way than had been tried before. This was the beginning of Wiconi International in Vancouver, Washington. This life-changing event would begin the journey that would influence the lives of many other Native leaders who sensed the same ministry vision. Richard and Katherine ministered through Wiconi from 1997 until Richard's passing in 2013.

In 1999 Wiconi began a major outreach with the formation of the Many Nations One Voice (MN1V) conferences held across the country. When these conferences were discontinued in 2004, Wiconi initiated their Family Camp. Every decision from one stage of the Wiconi life to the next was entered with discernment, confirmation, and prayer.

There was one last occasion in Richard's ministry when he spent time seeking the Lord's leading for Wiconi. Richard called together a core group of colleagues to spend a weekend in prayer and conversation about the future of Wiconi. From the results of that meeting, Richard made the decision to work more in his home community and do less traveling. This was a difficult choice to make because speaking engagements provided income. Richard did alter his direction and became more involved in his local community. This was one of the last major changes he made in Wiconi's ministry focus.

In 2009, Richard met J.R. Lilly, a gifted young Navajo man, acting as his mentor until 2012 when J.R. became his personal assistant. J.R. served Richard and the Wiconi organization well and helped Wiconi through the transition process.

The Next Season for Wiconi

Richard Twiss' passing left a large leadership gap in the Wiconi organization. Decisions had to be made about its future. This transitional time led us into a Liminal Phase where transition and change were necessary. But what would be the next stage for Wiconi?

For one year we ritually stayed in a state of 'limbo' by taking what is referred to in Native American traditions as the time of 'mourning for the death of a loved one'. The mourning period lasts for at least a year from the time of death, but sometimes for several years. During that year, many of Wiconi's local ministry leaders and followers participated in their Native mourning traditions, such as cutting one's hair and not saying the person's name. These are transitional periods when the time spent in a Liminal Phase (neutral zone) can allow us the opportunity to cope with immense changes.

In spite of our grief, we managed to make the 2013 Family Camp as enjoyable as possible, giving due respect to the life of Richard Twiss. When attending past Wiconi Family Camps, Richard always sat in the same chair during events in the auditorium. After his passing, we honored him by placing a blanket on his chair to represent his presence during our presentations and events. Further, while at the Powwow, we did the same and placed the blanket-covered chair in the Powwow circle. By doing this, we created traditional rituals to begin the transition to a Wiconi Family Camp/Powwow without our late leader.

Wiconi's 'in-between' time after Richard's death was exemplified by, 'We are not what we used to be and we are still becoming what we are not yet. In this in-between time we experience confusion, deep loss, fear, the unknown, searching and despair.'[1]

In January 2014, about one year after Richard's death, the current staff and board members, friends of Wiconi, and key contextual leaders gathered for a full weekend to deliberate about God's leading for the continuation of the main Wiconi ministries. We were encouraged by the scripture that affirmed that we believe God is able to do 'immeasurably more than all we ask or imagine, according to His power that is at work within us' (Eph. 3.20). We agreed to trust God and not to limit Him. We knew that there would be many more challenges in our future.

Looking for new leadership took some thoughtful planning. Throughout the year after Richard's death, I spoke to several people in Wiconi leadership and offered to help in any way to make sure that Wiconi International continued. I had already planned to work with the staff to help Wiconi Family Camp take place as scheduled that first year. During that time my secular job ended abruptly, leaving me unemployed.

As always in my life, the ending of one life situation clears the ground for a new beginning. Some transitions like this one are not planned – they just happen. Now here I am, the Director of Wiconi. I have been given a great opportunity. Sometimes you can work hard to create opportunities – other times everything is just given to you.

I am amazed when I look at the way the contextual ministry movement has spread and how I have grown in my understanding – upon realizing the process I had to travel through. Thus endings, Liminal Phases (neutral zones), and beginnings have a continual place in an organization's life cycle. Wiconi began as Richard Twiss' brain child. He took a stand and dreamed of an organization that could greatly impact the lives of Native Americans, their families, and communities – 'creating a preferred future'. The organizational transition Wiconi went through was monitored and planned by looking back at the past and forward to the future.

I must say something concerning a dream I had while pondering the changes and transitions involved with entering into ministry with Wiconi. I had been thinking about my place in Wiconi

---

[1] Twiss, 'Rescuing Theology from the Cowboys', p. 35.

and what it might mean to carry on Richard Twiss' vision of ministry. In the dream I met with Richard and we chatted for a while. Finally, I asked him, 'What should I do? How can I honor your life and legacy through my life as I help continue your life's work with Wiconi? He sat for a while and stared into the sky. Then he said these words to me:

> Case, all of life is a blessing from God. Make your family life a priority because your children will grow up so fast and be on their own before you know it. Don't take life so seriously, but take God very seriously. Enjoy your time working for the Lord, have some fun along the way, and enjoy the ride.

Migwetch (Thank you), Richard. I will!

BIBLIOGRAPHY

Alexander, Corky, *Native American Pentecost: Praxis, Contextualization, Transformation* (Cleveland, TN: Cherohala Press, 2012).

American Heritage College Dictionary (Boston, MA: Houghton Mifflin, 1985).

Barna, George, *Evangelism That Works* (Ventura, CA: Regal Books, 1995).

Bridges, William, *Managing Transitions: Making Sense of Life's Changes* (Boston, MA: Da Capo Press, 2004).

—*Managing Transitions: Making the Most of Change* (Boston, MA: Da Capo Press, 2009).

Chand, Samuel R. and Cecil B. Murphey, *Futuring: Leading Your Church Into Tomorrow* (Grand Rapids, MI: Baker Books, 2002).

Charisma House Staff and Passio Faith, *The Spiritual Warfare Bible: Modern English Version* (Lake Mary, FL: Charisma House, 2014).

Gilliland, Dean S., *Pauline Theology and Mission Practice* (Eugene, OR: Wipf and Stock Publishers, 1996).

Greenman, Jeffrey and George Kalantzis, *Life in the Spirit: Spiritual Formation in Theological Perspective* (Downers Grove, IL: InterVarsity Press, 2010).

Hayward, Douglas, 'The Foundation for Critical Contextualization: Preliminary Considerations for Doing Contextualization Among First Nations Christians', *Journal of North American Institute for Indigenous Theological Studies* 6 (2008), pp. 59-77.

Heifetz, Ronald A. and Marty Linsky, *Leadership on the Line: Staying Alive Through the Dangers of Leading* (Cambridge, MA: Harvard Business Review Press, 2013).

Heifetz, Ronald A., Marty Linsky and Alexander Grashow, *The Practice of Adaptive Leadership: Tools and Tactics for Changing Your Organization and the World* (Cambridge, MA: Harvard Business Review Press, 2013).

Hiebert, Paul G. and R. Daniel Shaw, *Understanding Folk Religion* (Grand Rapids, MI: Baker Academic, 2000).

Hiebert, Paul G., *Anthropological Insights for Missionaries* (Grand Rapids, MI: Baker Academic, 1986).

Hughes, Kerry, *The Incense Bible: Plant Scents That Transcend World Culture, Medicine, and Spirituality* (Philadelphia, PA: Haworth Press, 2007).

Hybels, Bill, *Courageous Leadership: Field-Tested Strategy for the 360° Leader* (Grand Rapids, MI: Zondervan, 2012).

Jenkins, Philip, *Dream Catchers: How Mainstream America Discovered Native Spirituality* (New York: Oxford University Press, 2004).

Johnston, Basil, *Ojibway Heritage* (Toronto, Ontario: McClelland & Stewart, 2011).

King, Roberta R., *Pathways in Christian Music Communication: The Case of the Senufo of Cote D'Ivoire* (Eugene, OR: Pickwick Publications, 2009).

LeBlanc, Terry, 'Culture, Faith and Mission: Creating the Future'. *The Journal of the North American Institute for Indigenous Theological Studies* 1 (2003), pp. 149-77.

Lingenfelter, Sherwood G., *Agents of Transformation: A Guide for Effective Cross-Cultural Ministry* (Grand Rapids, MI: Baker Academic, 1996).

—*Leading Cross-Culturally: Covenant Relationships for Effective Christian Leadership* (Grand Rapids, MI: Baker Academic, 2008).

—*Transforming Culture: A Challenge for Christian Mission* (Grand Rapids, MI: Baker Academic, 1998).

Mahdi, Louise C., Steven Foster and Meredith Little, *Betwixt & Between: Patterns of Masculine and Feminine Initiation* (Peru, IL: Open Court, 1987).

Mayhall, C. Wayne, 'Effective Evangelism: To Know Christ and to Make Him Known', *Christian Research Institute* 31.4 (2008).

McNeal, Reggie, *A Work of Heart: Understanding How God Shapes Spiritual Leaders* (San Francisco, CA: Jossey Bass, 2011).

Medicine, Beatrice and Sue-Ellen Jacobs, *Learning to Be an Anthropologist and Remaining Native: Selected Writings* (Champaign, IL: University of Illinois Press, 2001).

Neill, Stephen and the Rev. Owen Chadwick, *A History of Christian Missions* (New York: Penguin Books, 1990).

Nelson, Alan and Gene Appel, *How to Change Your Church (Without Killing It)* (Nashville, TN: Thomas Nelson Publishing Group, 2000).

Parks, Sharon D., *Leadership Can Be Taught: A Bold Approach for a Complex World* (Cambridge, MA: Harvard Business Review Press, 2013).

Plueddemann, James E., *Leading Across Cultures: Effective Ministry and Mission in the Global Church* (Downers Grove, IL: InterVarsity Press, 2009).

Pratt, Richard H., 'The Official Report of the Nineteenth Annual Conference of Charities and Correction, 1892', in *Americanizing the American Indians: Writings by the 'Friends of the Indian'* (Cambridge, MA: Harvard University Press, 1973), pp. 46-59.

Richardson, Rick, *Evangelism Outside the Box: New Ways to Help People Experience the Good News* (Downers Grove, IL: InterVarsity Press, 2009).

Robbins, Harvey and Michael Finley, *Why Change Doesn't Work: Why Initiatives Go Wrong and How to Try Again–And Succeed* (Albany, NY: Petersons, 1997).

Rogers, Everett, *Diffusion of Innovations* (New York: Free Press, 2010).

Roxburgh, Alan J., *The Missionary Congregation, Leadership, and Liminality* (New York: Bloomsbury Academic, 1997).

Smith, Craig Stephen and Bill McCartney, *Whiteman's Gospel* (Winnipeg, Manitoba: Intertribal Christian Communications, 1998).

Southerland, Dan, *Transitioning: Leading Your Church Through Change* (Grand Rapids, MI: Zondervan, 2002).

Turner, Victor, *The Ritual Process: Structure and Anti-Structure* (Piscataway, NJ: Transaction Publishers, Rutgers, 1969 reprinted 2008).

Twiss, Richard, *One Church, Many Tribes: Following Jesus the Way God Made You* (Ventura, CA: Regal Books, 2000).

—*Rescuing the Gospel from the Cowboys: A Native American Expression of the Jesus Way* (Downers Grove, IL: InterVarsity Press, 2015).

— 'Rescuing Theology from the Cowboys: An Emerging Indigenous Expression of the Jesus Way in North America' (DMin, Asbury Theological Seminary, Wilmore, KY, 2011).

van Gennep, Arnold, *The Rites of Passage* (London: Routledge, 1909).

Welker, Glenn, 'Chief Tecumseh Shawnee', *Indigenous People,* December 10. Accessed June 2015. http://www.indigenous peo ple.net/tecumseh.htm.

White, James Emery and L. Ford, *Rethinking the Church: A Challenge to Creative Redesign in an Age of Transition* (Grand Rapids, MI: Baker Books, 2003).

Whiteman, Darrell L., *Anthropology and Mission: The Incarnational Connection* (Chicago, IL: CCGM Publishing, 2003).

Zahniser, A.H. Mathias, *Symbol and Ceremony: Making Disciples Across Cultures: Innovations in Mission* (Federal Way, WA: MARC Publications, 1997).

Index of Biblical References

Index of Authors

About the Author

Dr. Casey Church is the Director of Wiconi International, a contextual Indigenous ministry based in Vancouver, Washington. He has a Bachelor of Science degree in Anthropology, a Master of Arts in Intercultural Studies, and a Doctor of Intercultural Studies. He is a Pokagon Band Potawatomi member from southwest Michigan. His Potawatomi name is Ankwawango, which means 'Hole in the Clouds'. He is of the Bear clan from his mother's side (the late Mary Church-Pokagon, a Pokagon Band Potawatomi member), and the Crane clan from his father's side (the late Leonard Church, Nottawasippi Huron Band). Casey, his wife Lora, and their five children have lived in Albuquerque, New Mexico, for the past fifteen years.

Casey's journey led him to study traditional spiritual teachings under his Anishinaabe elders. He investigated culturally-appropriate (contextual) approaches to Native evangelism at Fuller Theological Seminary. Casey and Lora pastored a Native church plant in Grand Rapids, Michigan, from 1996 to 2000. Their church was one of the first Native American contextualized congregations in the country. The Churches also ministered with Native Christian ministries in the Southwest.

Casey is a frequent presenter at national and regional conferences on Native ministry and is often asked to be a consultant, teaching his approach to contextual adaptation of Native rituals and ceremonies. He works with the Brethren in Christ Overcomers Alcohol Treatment Program in Farmington, New Mexico, conducting Christian Sweat Lodge Ceremonies and providing guidance in contextual ministry methods. He has served as a consultant and interim staff member for the General Board of Global Ministries of the United Methodist Church's Office of Native American and Indigenous Ministries.

Casey is a board member for NAIITS: An Indigenous Learning Community (previously the North American Institute for Indigenous Theological Studies), a contributing writer for its academic journal, workshop presenter at its symposiums and adjunct instructor at Portland Seminary in Newberg, Oregon.

Wiconi
Removing Barriers, Building Bridges

Learn more about Wiconi:

Wiconi
P.O. Box5246
Vancouver, WA 98668

Email: office@wiconi.com
Phone: 360-607-2599

Website: www.wiconi.com

www.ingramcontent.com/pod-product-compliance
Lightning Source LLC
Chambersburg PA
CBHW072349090426
42741CB00012B/2985